M000029044

DEDICATION

To the memory of Dr. Robert L. (Bob) Lindsey

The hand of the LORD was upon me, and he brought me out by the Spirit of the LORD and set me in the middle of a valley; it was full of bones. He led me back and forth among them, and I saw a great many bones on the floor of the valley, bones that were very dry. He asked me, "Son of man, CAN THESE BONES LIVE?"

I said, "O Sovereign LORD, you alone know."

Then he said to me: "Son of man, these bones are the whole house of Israel. They say, 'Our bones are dried up and our hope is gone; we are cut off.' Therefore prophesy and say to them: 'This is what the Sovereign LORD says: O my people, I am going to open your graves and bring you up from them; I will bring you back to the land of Israel. Then you, my people, will know that I am the LORD, when I open your graves and bring you up from them. I will put my Spirit in you and you will live, and I will settle you in your own land. Then you will know that I the LORD have spoken, and I have done it, declares the LORD.' "

Ezekiel 37:1-3 and 11-14

CAN THESE BONES LIVE?

AN EYEWITNESS ACCOUNT OF SPIRITUAL RENEWAL IN MODERN-DAY ISRAEL

BY

CHANDLER LANIER

Can These Bones Live?
Copyright © 2000 by W. Chandler Lanier
ALL RIGHTS RESERVED

All Bible references are from the New International Version of the Bible, copyright © 1973, 1978, 1984 by International Bible Society, Colorado Springs, Colorado. References marked KJV are from the Authorized King James Version of the Bible.

Fairmont Books is a ministry of The McDougal Foundation, Inc., a Maryland nonprofit corporation dedicated to spreading the Gospel of the Lord Jesus Christ to as many people as possible in the shortest time possible.

Published by:

Fairmont Books

P.O. Box 3595
Hagerstown, MD   21742-3595
www.mcdougalpublishing.com

ISBN 1-58158-026-6

Printed in the United States of America
For Worldwide Distribution

CONTENTS

PREFACE

Jewish people living in Israel today who have accepted Jesus Christ as Lord and Savior have little
difficulty in finding a Hebrew-speaking group with
which to worship. This has not always been so. The
following is an eyewitness account of the great
movement of the Holy Spirit which occurred in Israel during my thirty years there. The Holy Spirit
moved across denominational boundaries to bless
the entire Body of Christ, and few believers were
left unaffected. This is a record of how God chose to
move in many and often strange ways to bring about
this work of His Spirit in the land of Israel.

INTRODUCTION

The Holy Spirit began to make His presence felt in Israel in the late 1960s against a background of desperate needs, frustrated hopes and pathetic groping for the will of God. The thirty-six Christian denominations represented in Israel [1] were tightly secured in their denominational fortresses. Timidly, delegates of eighteen of these denominations came together once a year at the annual UCCI (United Christian Council in Israel) meeting in Tiberias. There, theological papers were presented (to be yawned over), endless committees were appointed, and everyone then retreated to his ecclesiastical barriers. We had all arrived in the country with our different backgrounds and policies, and while there was a cool politeness among Christians, there was not the trust and warmth that makes for real fellowship. The interdenominational relationships that did exist were rather like *"having a form of godliness but denying the power thereof"* (KJV). [2]

I remember, to my shame, that a dear brother of another denomination voiced a desire to have a joint observance of the Lord's Supper among all those present at one UCCI meeting. I refused, on vague doctrinal grounds. Afterwards, I felt a conviction in my heart that in rebuffing my brother's attempt to build unity in the group I had grieved the Holy Spirit.

I am a strong denominational man, loving my Southern Baptist heritage. I began to sense, however, that the Body of Christ transcends denominations to include all who walk hand-in-hand with the Lord Jesus Christ. I began to realize that one's loyalty to one's own denomination is not compromised by cooperating with other Christians.

When the handful of Jewish believers in Israel could be persuaded to attend these annual meetings, the Arab Christians would grumble. When, as happened one year, several Jewish believers used the meeting as an opportunity to voice their political differences with the Arabs, the fellowship of the group was completely destroyed. Jewish and Arab believers were united in one regard: they held a rather lightly veiled attitude toward expatriates of "Foreigner, go home." The Spirit of Christ hung bleeding on the cross of His fractured Church in Israel.

Then there was the matter of prayer. Many remarked during this period that there seemed to be a "brass dome" over the heavens, preventing their prayers from reaching God. Prayers just seemed to bounce back in our faces. As one whose prayer life had been rich and meaningful, I found this desert of prayer especially disconcerting.

One night in 1964, four couples living in the Tel Aviv area gathered at the Dugith Art Gallery [3] for a prayer meeting. What was envisioned was a short Bible study, an even shorter homily and a prayer or two. The whole thing was not to exceed an hour. These four couples were Roy and Florence Kreider and Paul and Bertha Swarr (Mennonites), Wayne and Carol King (members of Child Evangelism Fellowship) and Sallie and myself (Southern Baptists). These four couples had two things in common: we all were laboring under heavy crises in our lives, and we were all spiritually drained.

The Kings had been ordered out of Israel by the Ministry of the Interior. They had turned this way and that trying to find a way to stay in the country, but to no avail. When every other recourse failed, their parents had to come from the States to take care of their children. Wayne and Carol had to leave for Cyprus (where they continued their efforts to secure permission to remain in Israel). For weeks, their lawyer in Tel Aviv worked to reverse the government's decision while the Christian community upheld them in prayer. When all seemed lost, their visa was granted, provided they move to Nazareth. There was a feeling of victory, but it had come at the price of physical and emotional exhaustion.

The Kreiders had been heavily involved in the establishment of Nes Amin (Miracle of Nations), a Christian *kibbutz* near Acre. Things had not gone well at the settlement, and the pressure had mounted to such an extent that Roy and Florence were almost at the breaking point.

The Swarrs were engaged in a non-challenging tourist ministry which amounted to little more than simply meeting incoming tourists and arranging for accommodations and tours. Paul and Bertha were desperate for some sign from God that their ministry would be more meaningful and satisfying.

Sallie and I were undergoing intense persecution. We had arrived in Israel on March 29, 1961, with our four children and had spent the first year in language study in Natanya. Then we moved to Zahalah, a suburb of Tel Aviv, where many of the Israeli army officers lived. There was a strong anti-American bias in Israel at that time due to the aftermath of the 1956 War with Egypt. Israel had conquered the Sinai, but pressure from the United States forced Israel to give the Sinai back to Egypt.

The bulk of the persecution we suffered in those days was targeted at our two youngest children, who were then attending Israeli schools. The physical ill-treatment of our children continued for four years. The Lord would eventually give us victory, but the trial took its toll on our lives.

We were four couples, eight spiritual invalids, in danger of becoming casualties in *"the good fight of faith."*

We met that first night at Dugith, but the normal prayer meeting we had anticipated did not materialize. There was no Bible study, no singing, and no homily — just prayer. But what prayer it was! We were on our knees from 7:00 PM until midnight. We sensed something wonderful happening to us, and we basked in its glory.

The Holy Spirit simply took over. We felt His presence, and it was wonderful. We were refreshed, we were comforted, and we were healed.

This prayer meeting was definitely one of the roots of the Renewal that was to come. It was not, of course, the only one, and many other sources will be quoted. For me, however, it was the starting point.

In this historical record of the Renewal, I will include testimonies of many who experienced the Spirit's power. The names of the Jewish believers have been changed for, even today, they are often subjected to persecution by extremists. It is hoped that those coming to Israel in the future and seeing the fruits of the Renewal will know that preceding this harvest there was a long period of (as Winston Churchill expressed it so well) "blood, toil, tears and sweat."

Chandler Lanier
Clarksville, Georgia

§

CHAPTER ONE

THE ROOTS OF THE RENEWAL

THE ROOTS OF THE RENEWAL WERE MANY AND VARIED.

Jesus was witnessed to in the land of Israel long before the establishment of the State of Israel in 1948; of course He was. Baptists, both nationals and expatriates, had labored in the land since 1911, and we were just one denomination, and a very latecomer at that.

For hundreds of years, the Roman Catholics, Greek Catholics, Anglicans, Greek Orthodox, Coptics and the Church of Scotland — to name just a few — had labored sacrificially for the Lord in the land. All these had their institutions, which had healed, educated and ministered to both Arab and Jew faithfully through the years — even centuries. This, the building of institutions, could be referred to as "The Cycle of Institutionalization," and certainly must be considered one of the roots of the Renewal, as it afforded bases and support for those who were to follow.

There were invisible roots also. A great number

of followers of Jesus Christ labored in the land long before there was any evidence of renewal. Many of them, perhaps most of them, have been forgotten — except by God. The only evidence of their labors exists in some dusty archive. Many more lack even this tiny accolade to their faithfulness. The prayers, sacrifices and unrealized hopes of these saints, however, were as much a part of the Renewal as the more dramatic manifestations which were to follow. It was the fate of these faithful ones to sow without reaping, but their tears of frustration watered this soil. Their heartbreaking efforts were, in the eyes of the world, fruitless, yet they remain precious to the heart of God.

Dr. Baker James Cauthen, former executive secretary of the Board of Foreign Mission of the Southern Baptist Convention, now deceased, in a rather self-deprecating testimony (in view of his very large achievements), wrote of his own ministry. "I may not be allowed to ever harvest any fruit. I may not be allowed to cultivate that which has been planted. I may not even be able to plant, not even to plow the ground and make ready for the planting. But, please God, I will at least endeavor to remove a few rocks from the field." [4]

Considering such sacrificial lives, we might refer to them as a "Cycle of Tears." This may well have been the most meaningful cycle of all, for what plant grows without water, even the water of tears?

To bring the thought of "cycles" closer to the present, however, let us begin with the year 1961. Previous to this date, the efforts of the Evangelical Christians to witness for Jesus Christ in the land had been met with scorn by most Israelis. The Hebrew name for Jesus was *Yeshu*, which literally means "let his name be erased." Jesus, according to traditional Jewish thought, was a product of a Jewish woman and a Roman soldier. To their way of thinking, He had done none of the miracles attributed to Him by His disciples. Then Saul, a renegade Jew, changed his name to the Greek form, Paul. He appropriated the myth of Jesus' resurrection (Jesus' disciples had simply bribed the Roman guards and then stolen His body, of course) and founded this new religion.

Then, there came a subtle change in the attitude toward the person of Jesus in Israel. Perhaps the Holy Spirit used Jewish thinkers themselves to bring about the change. Martin Buber in his monumental poem, *Ich und Du* [5] (*I and Thou*), referred to Jesus as "my brother." In his *Two Types of Faith*,[6] Buber praised the faith of Jesus, laying on Paul the guilt of doing violence to what was, in reality, a godly life lived in the best Jewish tradition.

What followed was truly astounding. Jewish authors began to pour out books about Jesus, and none of them was insulting or derogatory. Many of these books expressed real appreciation for a Jesus who was part of Jewish history.

The life of Jesus began to be taught in Israeli public schools. He was presented as a "good Jew." He lived a godly life, went about doing good and never claimed to be either Messiah or God, as His foolish disciples taught. He ran afoul of the Roman authorities, who had Him put to death.

Donald Hagner summarizes this new Jewish attitude toward Jesus: [7] "The modern period has seen a drastic change in the Jewish appreciation of Jesus. The emergence of a positive attitude toward Jesus and His teachings, in light of the preceding centuries of disdain, is nothing less than astonishing. And that this positive attitude could be maintained through and beyond the Holocaust is something that must bring a spirit of repentance and gratitude to Christians." [8]

Hagner quotes Rabbi Maurice N. Eisendrath, president (in 1963) of the Union of American Hebrew Congregations (Reform Judaism): "But what about our Jewish attitude towards Christendom, towards Jesus, especially? Are we to remain adamant — orthodox — in our refusal to examine our own statements, our own facts, our own interpretations of the significance of the life of Jesus, the Jew? ... How long can we persist in ignoring his lofty and yet so simply stated prophetic and rabbinic teachings? ... How long before we admit that his influence was beneficial, not only to pagans, but to the Jews of his time as well?" [9] Perhaps this more liberal Jewish thinking toward the person of Jesus was being felt in many places of the world also, but it was especially true in Israel.

Many causes of this new thinking can be cited. First, the Holy Spirit seemingly was opening Jewish hearts to consider Jesus. Secondly, the Jew, being in his own country for the first time in two thousand years, felt free to investigate areas which he would have avoided when living in Gentile environments. Thirdly, the Israelis, especially the young people, during this period, were desperately seeking answers to the meaning of life. Whatever the reasons, it became easier, for a time at least, to speak, even teach about Jesus in Israel. This period could be termed "The Jesus Cycle," and it was in preparation for the coming Renewal.

There was a period in Israel in the middle of the 1960s and into the early 1970s when we Christians enjoyed a more relaxed atmosphere in which to present the Gospel of Jesus Christ. Certainly, the invitations to speak before secular Jewish groups and the opportunities to engage in earnest conversation with Jewish individuals suddenly burst upon us in a way that was completely unexpected. This writer, for instance, was able to engage in a dialogue with a staff member, Mr. Moshe Kohn, of the English newspaper *The Jerusalem Post*. Mr. Kohn had attacked an editorial I had written in the Baptist publication *Hayahad Digest*. My editorial and Mr. Kohn's rebuttal occupied an entire page in two issues of *The Jerusalem Post*. Such a dialogue had not occurred before in public print, at least to my knowledge, since the establishment of the State of Israel.

This "Jesus Cycle" was followed by a cycle in which the Holy Spirit made Himself felt across the land like a mighty wind. The Holy Spirit was the "catalyst" which brought all the elements of the Renewal together, shaking the Body of Christ in Israel to its foundations. This "Holy Spirit Cycle" occupies the major portion of this historical record, and is mentioned here only to place it in its historical perspective.

The "Holy Spirit Cycle" did not end, but there were two other cycles to follow. The "Cycle of Discipling" began to emerge. Many congregations in Israel developed discipling courses. The Immanuel House in Jaffa, for instance, established a study center, affording Bible studies in a live-in situation. The Norwegian Lutherans' Caspari Center in Jerusalem sponsored TEE (Theological Education by Extension), biblical studies by correspondence. The Baptists, in addition to their CSTC (Christian Service Training Center) in Haifa and a correspondence course, translated the discipling course *Masterlife* into Arabic and Hebrew. The response to these several training courses was overwhelming.

Finally, to complete the "cycle" motif, came a "Cycle of Persecution." This caused no small concern among believers. The Orthodox, for example, made an attempt to curtail Evangelical activity through legislation. Firm believers were not shaken by this. Joe Shulem, a *Sabra* (native-born Israeli) and a Jewish Christian representative of the Church of Christ denomination, saw beyond the persecution to a coming unprecedented growth of the Church in Israel. According to Shulem, the persecution was brought on by Orthodox circles being caught up in a wave of right-wing religious fanaticism sweeping throughout the Jewish community. This extremism was adopting a stance that said, "Observe Judaism in Orthodox worship or get out of the country." Such an attitude was alienating, not only to Arabs and Christians, but also to secular and Reform Jews as well.

Christians, Shulem states, endured this attack with patience and increasing commitment. By showing empathy toward the plight of suffering Jews in Russia and other countries, Christians earned the respect of Israelis who were not Orthodox and who were smarting under the pressure to conform. The Israe-

lis were drawing parallels between the hate-moti-
vated tactics of the Orthodox and the positive actions
of Christians, to the detriment of the former and the
advantage of the latter.

The fanatical elements, sensing the warming of the
general public toward Christians, reacted hysteri-
cally and used increasingly overt methods to force
the Israelis into line. Attempts to demand anti-missionary laws, which the government had been
reluctant to enforce, increased. The attempt to de-
fine who was a Jew was thought to be "the straw
that broke the camel's back." Israel had always held
an open-door policy for any and all persons who
were Jewish. The definition adopted by the government was "a Jew is anyone born of a Jewish mother."
Someone, therefore, who had a Jewish mother but
who had accepted Christ as Savior was still, by law,
a Jew. The Orthodox were denying that such a person was a Jew, and therefore he could not be eligible
to become an Israeli citizen.

The majority of Israelis, eighty-two percent, are
not Orthodox and resent this pressure. They are
seeking other ways to meet their spiritual needs, and
the Church is the beneficiary of this spiritual hunger.

This supposition of "cycles" is stressed in order
to confront two fallacies which are often expressed
in connection with the Renewal in Israel. The first
of these fallacies is that the renewal is to be credited

solely to the Charismatic Movement. While the Charismatic Movement played a leading role in the Renewal (as we shall see), the Renewal had many roots. The second fallacy is that of minimizing the contribution of the Charismatic Movement. It is a matter of record that the great majority of young people who came to the Lord during the Renewal were either in the Movement or were influenced by it. The Renewal had many roots, the Charismatic Movement being one of them, and a very important one. But the Movement was not the only root. After all, Jesus was a carpenter, and a carpenter uses many different tools. He sometimes finishes with one for the moment and proceeds to pick up another one. All of his tools are important for his task.

The Holy Spirit, knowing the honest reservations we had within the Body of Christ, demonstrated His loving concern for us in a marvelous way. Nothing in the Renewal is clearer than the evidence of the hand of God in the selection of those He chose to bring to Israel to guide us. The chapter entitled "The Tillers Arrive" will develop further the contribution of these guides.

That little prayer meeting at the Dugith Art Gallery in Tel Aviv mentioned in the Introduction was the beginning of the Renewal in that area. After the initial visitation of the Holy Spirit that first night, we began to meet weekly, remaining on our knees until midnight and beyond. Four hours seemed to us to be as four minutes, and there never seemed to be enough time for prayer. We always finished with a sigh of regret.

These sessions in prayer saved our ministries in Israel. The big "brass dome" was gone. We were "getting through" to God again. The meeting became the focal point of our week, the moment that we all waited for eagerly and impatiently. It was wonderful! It was glorious!

This wasn't "religion," nor was it "serving the Lord." This was something that the Holy Spirit was doing for us because He knew how desperately we needed to feel His presence in our lives.

It wasn't long before others began to notice the joy and excitement in our lives. This led to questions, which led, in turn, to many seeking to become part of our happiness. In this way, the group began to grow.

We began to meet in each other's homes. We decided, early on, not to turn these evenings into social occasions or even worship services, but to reserve this time solely for prayer. Answered prayer became a very common thing among us. We reported each week on how God had met this need or had solved that problem, and we praised Him for His faithfulness. Each week, we set new prayer goals, pointed ourselves toward new prayer targets and sought the Lord's leading in new directions.

More than the answered prayer, however, was the growing sense of the Holy Spirit in our lives. We wanted more. We could not get enough of Him! A few drops of the blessed presence of God's love had begun to fall on our lives, but we sensed that there was more ... much more ... to follow.

CHAPTER TWO

§

THE EARLY RAINS

THE PRAYER GROUP IN TEL AVIV GREW TO MANY TIMES ITS original size, and other such groups sprang up in Jerusalem, Haifa, Tiberias, Nazareth and Natanya. In all of these groups, the denominational factor simply did not play a part. If some visitor had inquired as to the denominational affiliation of those attending, the reply, in all probability, would have been, "Why, I don't know. It never occurred to me to ask."

The best description, perhaps, of what was happening was given by General Ralph Haines, Jr., a participant from America in the "World Conference on the Holy Spirit" held in Jerusalem on March 2-5, 1974. General Haines said: "It is like a lot of ducks swimming around in various pools. The Baptists swim in their pool, the Presbyterians swim in their pool, the Methodists in their pool, etc. Now the Holy Spirit is pouring down His love on all these little pools until they overflow their banks, and the ducks from all the little pools begin to swim together in one great pool of God's love."

And so we were. We were not so much forgetting denominational differences as pooling together the strengths that these backgrounds afforded us. We were united in one joyous chorus of praise to God, who was doing *"a new thing"* right before our very eyes. The first great fruit of the Renewal, then, was the removal of the barriers between denominational groups in Israel, affording free and open fellowship between believers.

The second blessing of the Renewal was even more dramatic. Mention has been made previously of the tension between the few Jewish Christians and those of us who were expatriates. We had come to Israel hoping to be accepted by them and to work closely with them for the good of Christ's Kingdom. The tension between us, however, had prevented this from happening. The Renewal greatly reduced this tension, and native and foreigner became one in the Lord. It is rather thrilling how the Holy Spirit accomplished this miracle.

The number of Jewish believers had grown considerably, but this growth was not a natural one among Jewish believers already in the country. God began to bring to Israel Jews who had met the Lord through organizations such as Jews For Jesus, Youth With A Mission, Campus Crusade and others. Other Jews who came had been saved directly out of their lost conditions without the intervention of any other

Christians. It was a sovereign work of the Holy Spirit. Some of these had not had any contact with Christians or Christianity at all. Christ had simply met them where they were. Many of these people had been lifted out of drugs, out of organized crime or out of cults, and each individual had a thrilling testimony to give of the reality of Jesus Christ in his or her life.

These Jews also shared another reality. God had called them to leave their homes in other countries and to come home to Israel. They came knowing next to nothing about the doctrines and history of Christianity. They were ignorant of the dogmas and tiny niceties of the faith which often tend to divide rather than unite the faithful. They knew that they had met the Lord and that He was theirs and they were His. They busied themselves praising His name with such vigor that those of us who were un-accustomed to such exuberance often felt rather nonplused.

On hearing of the prayer groups in the country, these new Jewish believers migrated happily to them, and there they found a warm welcome. Suddenly, there was a relaxed feeling of acceptance among believers, Jewish and non-Jewish alike. The tensions of the past were gone, and trust took their place.

Expatriates soon found themselves welcomed to

attend the meetings of the Jewish believers, and in many cases they were even invited to join. This change in attitude was nothing short of a miracle. Those of us who had gazed with longing eyes for any sign of acceptance by those we had come to serve marveled at the power of God that was at work. The very real barriers between local believers and expatriates had been broken down.

As the winds of the Holy Spirit began to stir our hearts, there were granted to some visions of what was to come. Roy Kreider shares an account of such a vision: "One evening, while listening to a live concert in a small assembly hall, a graphic scene came suddenly into view. Before me, I saw the broad expanse of the Negev Desert, its thirsting sands, its parched gravel and bald rocks glistening in the fierce summer sun. A deep, dry *wadi* yawned to the left, stretching toward a lifeless plain. My attention was riveted to the embankment before me, which, as I watched, began to heave and lurch as by some powerful force beneath it.

"The sands soon turned dark and muddy as the mud-swirl thickened and suddenly tumbled over the side into the *wadi* as a swelling mudflow. When the muddiness cleared away, a strong fountain bubbled forth, rising into an artesian well. Sweeping mud before it, the rising torrent quickly filled the *wadi* with clear water flowing strongly toward the dry plain beyond.

"With the muddiness gone, a remarkable transformation occurred. The banks of the *wadi* broke out with greenery. The plain beyond, as by a miracle, became an orchard of fruit-bearing trees. Among the trees, dressed in heavenly blue and moving with great energy and joy, the Fruit Gatherer was selecting ripened fruit.

"My vision revealed a process that was already unfolding. When the thirst had reached a point of desperation, the fountain had broken out. The movement in that enormous amount of mud was itself a sign of new beginnings through a process of cleansing. Only when the pure stream came forth did the landscape change and the fruitfulness appear. The action of the mud was impressive, but my attention was drawn even more to the power that caused the action. The churning of the mud was only the prelude to the fountain bursting into full view. The transformation and fruitfulness of the desert was a miracle of divine power, a joyful work of the Lord.

"I recognized the vision as a parable of my own experience. The Lord has dealt gently with me, drawing me to Himself gradually, enfolding me and enabling me to follow step-by-step as He leads me on. I have not experienced the Holy Spirit through startling manifestations or a sudden invasion of my life. He has never crashed into my consciousness in a dramatic manner. Rather, in a beautiful way, He enlarges what He has earlier given me. From regeneration onward, I have known the Holy Spirit as He draws, encourages, convicts and constrains me. He is always leading me closer to the Father and deeper into the full-orbed life of Jesus." [10]

From the beginning of the Renewal, lives were being changed. Sarah Bivins tells of how Jesus touched her life: "We arrived in Israel in October of 1961 and went directly to the Baptist Village to live. We had one daughter, Lynn, ten months old, and two more daughters were to be born to us there in Israel — Simone Beth in 1963, and Ruth Ann in 1965. It seemed that all I was doing was taking care of the three girls and cleaning house. I wasn't doing anything that I had come to Israel to do, and I was constantly down in the dumps. I loved the Lord, but there wasn't any power in my life.

"I was also having a difficult time with our second daughter. She would hold her breath for an extended period, go into convulsions and pass out. This was very frightening to me. I heard of a prayer group and asked a friend to have the group pray for our daughter. Later, he told me that they had prayed and that he felt that she would be completely well. Interestingly enough, she began to get better. When we went on furlough and she was examined by a doctor, she was found to be completely normal.

"On the night of June 13, 1966, I had finished my

work and was sitting on the balcony reading John Sherrill's book *They Speak With Other Tongues*. He said that he had been determined not to raise his hands when he prayed, and that was exactly what the Lord required him to do before he was blessed with the Holy Spirit. I was alone that night, and very gingerly I raised my hands a little bit and whispered, 'Praise the Lord.' Nothing happened.

"I got down on my knees and started saying to the Lord, 'Lord, I am completely worthless without You.' Then I began praying the Lord's Prayer in Spanish, then in English and then in Hebrew. Every time I reached the part of the prayer that says, 'Thy Kingdom come,' I would add, 'in me, Lord. I want Your kingdom to come in me.'

"As I continued to pray, I became aware of God's presence. His love flowed over me. I felt that I was lifted up beyond time and space into God's presence, and I knew what John meant when he said that *God is love*. I was being filled to overflowing with the love of God.

"Then suddenly I realized that I was hearing in my mind certain words in a language I could not recognize. I repeated the words out loud, and as I did, I felt a great joy bubbling up inside of me. I knew that God was aware of my love for Him, and I knew that God loved me.

"God told me to take the book to Eddie Fields. She

was busy, but someone else was there who said, 'Sarah, you look especially pretty today.' I felt like I was glowing all over.

"After that, the Lord began to give me little instructions to do certain things. I was to go to the closet and pray, for instance, and I would be obedient and do it. He would tell me to clean house and to bake a cake, and as soon as I finished the cake, someone would come who would appreciate a clean house and a piece of cake.

"One time, I was at a nonkosher butcher shop, and the Lord told me to buy nine pork chops. *Why nine chops?* I wondered, but I bought them anyway. That was on Friday. The next day, which was our day of worship in Israel, Ilana and Paul Hoedlzley came to church for the first time and brought another couple with them. I asked them to come to dinner and they consented. The four of them and the five of us had nine pork chops that day."[11]

These "Early Rains" changed many people, not only spiritually, but physically and mentally. For some, it meant the finding of God's will for their lives. Bob and Eddie Fields, for instance, received guidance from God for Bob's life. Here is how Bob recalled what happened: "During the summer of 1971, I became restless and wanted to return to the States to build a retreat center. I decided to fast, something that I had never done before. I borrowed a friend's apartment (he was out of the country at the time) and spent that weekend in fasting and prayer. I didn't know what to expect, but something very important to my ministry occurred. The Lord caused me to see that there was nothing wrong in my yearnings, that I was a complete and acceptable person in His sight. He let me know that this desire to return to the States and build a retreat center was from Him. The firstfruits of the Renewal, for me at least, was discovering God's will for my life.

"The second was a 'gift of grace.' The idea of up-rooting and returning to the States without any visible income was a rather disturbing one. We would have to learn to depend solely on God's faith-fulness to provide all our needs. We had to learn that it was not enough to have a task to perform. It was not enough, either, to have the gift to perform that task. The gift and the task had to come together under God's timing." [12]

So it went. Like an autumn wind blowing dry leaves, our lives began to feel the cool breezes of the Holy Spirit. The ground was being made ready for the coming of the tillers

Chapter Three

&

The Arrival of the Tillers

God began to bring to Israel in the late 1960s certain individuals whom I call "the tillers" because they prepared the soil of our hearts by instructing us in the things of the Spirit. At first, there were just one or two of them, but then the trickle grew into a steady stream.

It was interesting that each teacher usually had only one truth to emphasize, so that we were able to absorb that teaching before being confronted by another. These teachers all taught from personal experience. What they had received from the Lord, they shared with us. There was nothing secondhand about their witness.

The tillers came, they taught and then they left. Others came to do the same — teach and then leave. The Holy Spirit, like a master carpenter, would reach for one tool, use it, set it aside and then reach for another.

Looking back now, the pattern is clear ... and very beautiful.

The first of those who would come were the Phillips, Aubrey and Dorothy, from England. Aubrey was sent to Israel as field manager for BOAC Airlines. It was the delightful English reserve of the Phillips and the beauty of their lives which attracted us to them. It was not until their tour of duty in Israel was finished and they had returned to England that we learned that the Phillips had experienced certain gifts of the Spirit. They had sensed, and rightly so, that out group was not yet ready to receive teachings concerning these gifts. What they did teach us was the necessity of praise in our lives. In their gentle quietness, they kept us from dissolving into frothy emotionalism while strengthening a solid expression of wonder and love toward God.

Concerning this same quietness in which the Lord allowed us to be led, Bertha Swarr writes: "Life in this new dimension has its moments of ecstasy, but it is mostly a cool, calm walk of faith, in moment-by-moment obedience to the inner promptings of the Spirit, constantly checked and in agreement with the written Word, and in subjection to and conjunction with fellow members of the Body of Christ, and through whomever God chooses to speak." [13]

John and Yvonne Childers of Auckland, New Zealand, shared this parable: "In one area of the evergreen forests, in New Zealand, at a certain time of maturing, the falling needles cause a chemical reaction on the mineral-rich soil which produces a hard crust. Before long, this surface becomes impenetrable to the rains. As the soil becomes dry, trapping the minerals underneath, plant growth is stunted. The remedy is to open the subsoil to fresh air. Then the sun and the rain are able to do their work again, and the plants flourish. The personal lessons in this parable are obvious. Adverse responses and attitudes create an insensitivity to the Holy Spirit and block fresh things of God from getting through to us." [14]

Rev. David Pawson was pastoring a large church in England. He felt led, not to leave the church, but to lead the congregation into breaking up into smaller "house groups" in which the Holy Spirit could act in a more intimate way. The result had been a phenomenal growth in the congregation, not only in numbers but also in the depth of its spiritual commitment. Pastor Pawson's experience with such groups was shared with the Church in Israel and took hold. In Israel today, house groups play a vital role in the life of the believers.

Richard Beals, a Methodist minister from Kentucky, came to Israel and taught on the work of the Holy Spirit in the life of Jesus and on the discipline of fasting. This was a completely new area to most of us.

Bob Dollars, who had served as a Southern Baptist volunteer in Africa, was a special help to Bob and Eddie Fields. Eddie relates: "Bob prayed a very strange prayer. He prayed that God would assure Bob that he was very much in God's service. That was great. But then he prayed for me. He prayed that I would not be a hindrance to what Bob wanted to do and that I would not stand in his way. This was very strange because I had always supported Bob in whatever he wanted to do.

"However, I had been in deep depression from feeling that my life had many 'loose pieces' that were 'floating around,' and that life wasn't making sense. Bob's prayer brought to light the reason for this depression (objection to my husband's dream of leaving Israel and building a retreat). The prayer brought all the 'loose pieces' together into a healthy whole. Suddenly, I felt peace, wonderful peace." [15]

Millions of people in many countries heard Corrie Ten Boom speak, and it was a special thrill for me to sit with this great lady and hear her tell of her experiences with the Lord. No one could be the same after meeting her. She was the author of *No Good If Detached*, *Amazing Grace*, *Tramp for the Lord* and other books which told of her persecution in Nazi Germany and the death of her sister in a concentration camp. Israel was also blessed by her ministry.

John Kershaw, Faid Karmout (a Baptist pastor)

and Costa Deir (a Greek Orthodox) — three Arabs (all born in Ramle, Israel) — brought us teachings on casting out demons, healing and prophecy. These teachings were in no way dogmatic or threatening, but were delivered in the sense: "If this is for you, grasp it." They simply related what they had experienced.

In the early 1970s, whole teams of teachers began to arrive. The most important of these had four members, one of them being Costa Deir. The group was sent to us by MAP (Missionary Assistance Program) of California, whose president was Ralph Mahoney, and he was also a member of the team. These men conducted meetings, mainly at the Anglican Retreat Center (Stella Carmel) near the Druse Village of Isafia, near Haifa.

Costa Deir was a very colorful character, having led a rather checkered life before coming to the Lord. He had been a professional wrestler (which in itself serves to describe him). Not tall, but very broad and barrel-shaped, he was immensely strong. He sported a little mustache which twirled up to a sharp point at each end and which he kept neatly waxed. This man radiated joy and happiness as naturally as a potbellied stove radiates heat, and his perpetual smile could have melted ice.

All four members of the team were remarkable,

in that one or the other of them could appeal to almost everyone they ministered to. I immediately
identified with Ralph Mahoney. As quiet and calm
as Costa Deir was exuberant, he was also disciplined
and fine-tuned in his terminology. He played on my
heartstrings like a harpist in full concert.

It was Ralph Mahoney whom I first heard speak
of the Renewal as being like a fish. A fish has bones,
he reminded us. If one of the teachings (speaking in
tongues, for instance) was to stick in our throats, we
should simply pull it out and cast it away. It wasn't
for us. He warned us, however, not to miss the fish,
not to miss all that God was doing because we did
not find every point appealing. We could not afford
to miss the new thing the Holy Spirit was bringing
to pass in the land of Israel.

Ralph told us that his nature (like my own) was
to be very questioning. He related instances of how
one presentation of Renewal truths by the team had
succeeded "beyond belief" in one country, while that
same presentation had gone over "like a lead bal-
loon" in another. Each time, after much prayer and
searching, God had revealed to them an approach
that would break through to men's hearts.

He told us that in Africa the team had used a very
emotional witness — the more enthusiasm, singing
and shouting, the better. The people responded by

the thousands. Using that same approach in Japan, however, had brought absolutely no response, and the team had even considered giving up and moving to another country. When it was his turn to speak one night, he felt not only discouraged, but also rather angry — with the audience and with God.

He remembered, "I determined, almost in spite, to be as dry as possible, and I spoke on the philosophy of Anselm — my field. About halfway through my talk, the audience came alive, and the people were so animated that they even rose to their feet to applaud. You never know. Different people, different responses."

As Ralph spoke that night, my heart melted within me, my soul was fed and my parched spirit drank deeply as I encountered the Holy Spirit. When this happened, I realized that it had happened twice before. The first time I had been in a hotel room, and the Lord called me out of the business world and into the ministry. The second time happened not long after that. I was driving a bus to Oklahoma to show it (my business at the time was selling buses), when I began to feel the presence of Christ in the bus. I felt it for the better part of the next several hundred miles.

There was a difference between the two experiences. With the first, in the hotel room, there had been an overpowering feeling of awe, knowing that the Holy Spirit was there in the room and dealing with me. This was not altogether a pleasant sensation, for I felt that while God loved me, He was concerned that I was "drifting" with no real spiritual goal in life. I was under such conviction that I could not enjoy His presence. The second instance was much lighter and, perhaps, less profound. It was, however, delightful, as one delights in the presence of a loved one. It was fellowship with Jesus on the highest level, and it was wonderful. Joy and praise bubbled out of me in scripture, prayer and singing. It was great!

The experience at Stella Carmel, however, differed from the other two in several aspects. I felt (actually felt) healing inside of me. I felt as if I was being accepted, that somehow God was pleased with me and that I need not fear anything anymore.

My experience with the Holy Spirit that night was not accompanied by speaking in tongues or other manifestations, but I knew that it was real. In the days that followed, many began to press me to know the details of the experience, and some, learning that it was not accompanied by the same gifts they had received, doubted its validity. God gave me enough peace not to argue with them. I had entered that state of knowing (not of salvation, for that certainty had been mine for thirty years already) of which Augustine spoke when he said, "I do not believe because I know; I know because I believe."

The tillers kept coming in goodly numbers. After preparing the ground, they sowed seed and they carefully cultivated. Those who were experiencing the things of the Spirit in Israel ceased to be counted as isolated cases and now came in ever-growing numbers.

CHAPTER FOUR

§

THE GIFTS BROUGHT BY THE RENEWAL

ALTHOUGH THE CHARISMATIC MOVEMENT WAS JUST ONE tool among many which God used to bring about the Renewal, I am grateful for its contributions and praise its strengths. The "mainline" denominations have clearly erred when they have refused to explore the new and unknown. To whom can God turn when the larger and more heavily endowed denominations refuse to step out in faith to tread new paths? Does He have any other choice than to work through those who are willing to launch out into the deep?

The gifts of the Spirit often referred to by Charismatics are recorded in Paul's first letter to the Corinthians (see 1 Corinthians 12:4-10). There are nine of them: the word of wisdom, the word of knowledge, faith, healing, miracles, prophecy, discerning of spirits, tongues and interpretation of tongues. However, in his letter to the Romans, Paul listed seven other gifts: prophecy, serving, teaching, exhortation, giving, leading and mercy (see Romans 12:6-8). Then, in Ephesians 4:11, five more are listed:

apostles, prophets, evangelists, pastors and teachers. It can be said that God has given as many "gifts" as there are needs to be met.

Even the nine gifts of the Spirit listed in 1 Corinthians 12 are interpreted differently by various Christian groups. For example, is the word of wisdom to be understood (as some think) to mean a timely thought expressed by someone through experience or natural sagacity? Or, is it (as other Christians believe) a sudden flash of insight given supernaturally by the Spirit at an opportune time for the edification of the Body? Is a word of knowledge to be understood as simply teaching, or is it a supernaturally given word of truth in a given situation? Is prophecy knowing the future, or is it boldly preaching the message of Christ? Is discerning of spirits a supernatural gift which enables one to recognize and exorcise demons, or is it the innate ability of a person whose sensitivity allows him or her to reach through another's disguise to get to the core of the problem? Is speaking in tongues a supernatural expression of one's spirit to God through words that are at the same time a language and yet not a language (at least in the sense of a language that can be understood), or is it simply speaking subliminal words of praise from the subconscious? Is interpretation of tongues translating that which cannot be understood when someone speaks in a spiritual language, or is it simply the verbalization of an impulse following such an expression?

The gifts listed in Romans 12 and Ephesians 4:11 are apparently straightforward ministries. Some Christians, therefore, speak only of "the nine gifts of the Spirit," rather than including those in Romans and Ephesians, and sincere Christians, sincerely expressing their interpretation of the gifts, have sometimes caused division. The evidence of the Renewal is that this need not be the case. There is room for every gift.

The fact is that there are many gifts that do not appear in the lists given in the Bible. [16] One of these came to me. I had a dream about a bridge. The meaning of the dream eluded me, but the dream kept occurring night after night, until I eventually became rather unsettled at the fact that I could not grasp the meaning. I decided to undertake what was to me a new discipline — that of fasting. During the next few days, I took only water as I sought the Lord for the meaning of the dream. After three or four days of fasting and prayer about the matter, it became clear to me that *I* was to be the bridge.

But a bridge between whom? And for what purpose? I did not yet know the answer to those questions.

About that time, there was a serious problem brewing in the congregation I was attending at the

Baptist Village. The rift between those who were open to the rapidly growing Renewal and its accompanying gifts and those who were suspicious of it, even hostile to it, was threatening a serious split in the church. Just then, I was approached by the pastoral committee of the congregation and asked to become the pastor. As I weighed my decision in this matter, suddenly the meaning of the bridge in my dreams became clear. God wanted me to act as a bridge between the two factions in the congregation.

Having recently had an experience with the Holy Spirit, I was in a position to understand those who were having similar occurrences. At the same time, having had the experience without the accompaniment of speaking in tongues (the specific sign that many were looking for), I was able to empathize with those who had not yet encountered these phenomena and was able to reassure them that they were in no way second-class Christians. I encouraged them to flow with the Holy Spirit without fear and to glean from the Renewal all that the Spirit was offering without believing anything that violated their convictions. I urged them not to feel pressured, and to reject it if others tried to force it upon them. My particular spiritual gift, at that moment, then, was to serve as the bridge between believers of differing experiences so that the love of Christ could continue to flow among us.

Through the mercy of God, this is exactly what happened in the days ahead. God helped us to pull together the various factions, the love of Christ was preserved, and a split was avoided. Was this a unique gift only for a unique time? It may have been in our case, but when the Holy Spirit begins to work in any congregation, divisions are almost inevitable, and someone is needed to serve as a bridge between believers.

A very different spiritual gift was granted to Eddie Fields. Her gift was the removal of fear and hate from her life. "Is this a spiritual gift?" some might ask. She thinks so. She said: "On furlough in 1967, I was suffering so from my back that I had to spend much time in bed. Then I began to have trouble with my heart. I had always determined to try to be like Jesus, so I had covered up every response of anger or distrust and had not allowed myself to experience the venting of my true feelings. I prayed, and the Holy Spirit began to show me that there was hatred in my heart. I was shocked because I felt that I loved everyone and couldn't think of anyone that I hated. He showed me that conflicts with my fellow Baptist workers had caused a residue to form in my heart, and He showed me that I hated an Arab laborer at the Baptist Village.

"In a dream, I saw myself walking with this man from the road into the Baptist Village, about half a mile. As we walked, we were hitting each other and screaming at each other. The man screamed, 'I hate you! I hate you! You Western woman.'

"I was so disturbed by this dream that I immediately got out of bed and began to pray. My heart was pounding within me. As I asked God's forgiveness for the hate that I had held in my heart for this man, my heart began to slow down to its normal rhythm.

"I was reminded of another episode that had upset me when we were living in Natanya. A neighbor entered our apartment when Bob was not there, threw me on the bed and held me down. I was terrified and kept saying, 'Jesus loves you.' In the end, nothing happened, but I had been terrified of the man ever since. Now, I had to ask the Lord to remove this fear from my heart.

"One night, the Lord awakened me and showed me in letters like a neon sign on the bedroom wall: 'Relate to Me and, as I need you, I will send you.' In these words, the letter 'I' stood out brightly.

"We were on furlough a year and a half, and though we wanted to return to the Baptist Village, we were assigned to East Jerusalem. I felt a tremendous pull in my spirit, trying to identify first with the needs of the Jews and also with the needs of the Arabs. This wish to be a reconciler between Jew and Arab brought me to my lowest spiritual depths. It happened in this way:

"I kept thinking, *If I love these people so much, surely*

God loves them even more, and surely He has something for them beyond Jesus. I didn't realize it at the time, but these thoughts opened the way for powers of darkness to rush in with doubts of the divinity of Jesus. This was followed by a coldness and an emptiness in my heart and a great fear. I tried to push these doubts out of my mind through prayer, but it just didn't work. I told Bob that we would have to resign if I couldn't get back in touch with Jesus.

"I went to a Christian ladies' retreat. When the group decided to take a trip to Ein Gev, I told them to go without me. I was feeling very low and depressed. I had come to the conclusion that life without Jesus was not worthwhile.

"I went up on the rooftop of the building where we were staying, fell on my face before God and begged Him to reveal Himself to me. I was asking to see Jesus. What motivated me to do this was an experience a very dear friend had related to me. She had been badly burned and was placed on pain-controlling drugs. Her doctor warned her that the drugs were very addictive and that she should use them as little as possible, but she found herself becoming addicted to them because her pain was so terrible that she couldn't bear it without the help of the drugs. She cried out to God to help her. One night, in the midst of her pain, Jesus appeared by her bedside and comforted her. She was able to overcome her pain without becoming addicted to the drugs.

"This experience encouraged me to cry out to God now for that same comforting, and it worked. On the rooftop that day, God's Spirit was manifested to me, and the feelings of depression began to lift. I was able to praise God again. In the days that followed, the wonderful, incomprehensible peace I was feeling continued. Now, I trace all these things — restoration of faith in Jesus, loss of fear and being able to relax — back to my experience with the Holy Spirit." [17]

Having concluded that the list of spiritual gifts can be enlarged beyond the nine given in 1 Corinthians 12, let us consider the more demonstrable gifts among that list, particularly tongues and interpretation of tongues. Speaking in tongues, according to my personal observation, occurs among believers in three different situations. The first happens when believers are alone, praying to God. Tongues becomes a sort of extra dimension to their prayer, a means of entering into a deeper relationship with God. Because of this, many believers refer to this gift as "my prayer language." Those who practice the gift of tongues in private prayer often remain silent concerning its use and may even be reluctant to discuss it. There are many believers who pray in this manner, unbeknownst to others.

The second instance where tongues appears is in small groups of believers who are worshipping. In this case, tongues may become a part of their worship. Here again, there is sometimes little discussion of the experience outside the group.

The third occasion for the manifestation of the gift of tongues occurs in very large meetings. During the process of the service, one or more people will give a message (just like a prophecy) in tongues. This is followed by an interpretation of what has been said. I have been present so many times when these last two manifestations have occurred that I no longer find the practice disturbing or consider it unacceptable in any way. Many of those Jewish believers brought into faith through the Renewal received this gift. Many of the Christian expatriates were also endowed with it.

In a rather humorous way, Lee Bivins relates how he received this gift: "The Lord sent people from time to time to teach us what they had been experiencing in their own lives with the Holy Spirit. I learned these lessons and began to pray for the indwelling of the Holy Spirit. It happened to me one night as I lay in bed. I was singing an old German song, *"O Mein Papa."* As I was singing along, suddenly I began to sing in a new tongue.

"I will have to admit that I have often wondered what the value of speaking in tongues was. It did teach me one great lesson, however, and that is that I can trust God in all things — even with the control of my tongue." [18]

A great percentage of those being touched by the

Renewal received the gift of tongues. It is a legitimate supernatural manifestation, a touch of the Holy Spirit upon the lives of God's people. To those who would question its reality and remonstrate with those who practice it, I can only say that I have witnessed too many whom I respect and know of their devotion to Christ who have this gift to doubt its validity.

At the same time, for other believers such as myself, who have received gifts of the Spirit, but not speaking in tongues or some other particular one, we must never think that we are second-class Christians because our gifts differ. God knows what He is doing, and He knows what gifts to give and to whom.

Concerning the gift of prophecy through a message in tongues, it seems to me that, without exception, when such a prophecy has been given in a public meeting in which I have been present, the content of the prophecy was one of hope and encouragement. Very often, the prophecy was a statement that God loves His people and that He will not forsake them. Surely God does love us, and it is a good thing for us to be reminded of this fact as often as possible.

Healing miracles were among the first of the manifestations of the Spirit to be evidenced among us. The first healing occurred in the Bivins' living room. There were twelve present in the prayer group that

Sabbath night, and one of them was Mrs. Mary Smith, about seventy years old, from England. Mrs. Smith had suffered a fall six years previously that had left her back stiffened, and she could not bend over. She was able to walk, but she had to do so (as well as sit and lie down) with her back absolutely straight. Even then, she was in constant pain.

Paul Swarr relates what happened: "On a Sabbath afternoon in 1970, twelve persons had gathered in a living room at the Baptist Village. We were discussing the implications of Agnes Sanford's book *The Healing Gifts of the Spirit*. Someone said, 'If we truly believe that God's power is available today as it was to Peter and John, why don't we pray right now for the healing of Mrs. Smith's back?'

"We circled around Mary Smith and began to pray. I joined with the others, but I did not really expect anything to happen. I had never been taught to ask God for miracles.

"Then Mary Smith suddenly cried out, 'I am healed! I am healed!' I was startled. Amazed, I opened my eyes.

" 'Help me to my feet,' Mary demanded, and in less than a minute, the lady with the stiff back was touching the floor with the palms of her hands! My mind was boggled, and my thoughts were jammed. I had just witnessed a first-century miracle.

"Spontaneously, we all prayed and praised God, rejoicing and shouting, 'Blessed be the Lord God of

Israel, who does wondrous things. Hallelujah!' That miracle was the key that opened the door for me into a whole new realm of faith. Now I know that God is able, miraculously and instantaneously, to pour His healing power into a human body even in the twentieth century.

" 'This miracle was not merely for me,' Mrs. Smith told us, 'but so the Body of Christ here in Tel Aviv will grow in faith.' And that is exactly what began to happen." [20]

In the days after that, the miracles of healing continued unabated. A TWA pilot's wife, previously unknown to any of us, was deathly sick with peritonitis. She was anointed with oil in her hospital bed by the Anglican priest while the community of believers prayed in their homes. She recovered so rapidly that the hospital staff was astonished.

A young Jewish boy, struck by a car while riding his motorcycle, had been in a coma for more than two weeks. One of the believers was led to go to the hospital and pray for him, and the next day he was off the critical list.

Dale and Anita Throne served in Nazareth. In 1971, Anita had contracted a strange disease that doctors could not identify. As Anita became sicker, her doctors feared for her life. A co-worker expressed his shock on seeing Anita's condition. "If I had been a Roman Catholic priest, I would have administered Extreme Unction," he said.

Ray Register felt that God wanted him to pray for Anita's healing. He later wrote: "Rev. Fuad Sackhnini (pastor of the Nazareth Baptist Church), George Laty (one of the deacons) and I went to the hospital at ten-thirty one night. We anointed Anita with oil and prayed for her recovery. The next morning, she awoke feeling so well that, although her doctors insisted that she stay in the hospital for two more days, she got out of bed and went home." [20]

Dr. Robert L. Lindsey, senior Baptist representative in Israel and pastor of the Jerusalem Baptist Church, began to include in his services a time for the sick to come forward to be healed. Among the miracles he witnessed were these: a blind man recovered his sight, a man with a short leg had that leg extended to equal the other leg, deaf people regained their hearing and demons were cast out of people.

By this time, the Renewal was in full swing, and manifestations of the gifts of the Spirit had become quite common. Were they the main fruit of the Renewal? Some would reply, "Certainly," but I'm not sure that is true. The manifestations were definitely important, for they increased the faith of believers. Robert Lindsey gives them, especially the healings, the credit for increasing the size of his congregation from "about twenty on a good day" to three hundred and fifty to four hundred each weekend.

The manifestations were certainly an integral part

of the Renewal, but were they the most significant part? When we say that Jesus performed many *"signs and wonders,"* we use the word *oth* in Hebrew. This word has the meaning of a sign pointing to something as, for instance, a road sign points to a town. The miracles of Jesus pointed to His divinity. Through them the people realized that He was a person of authority. The miracles He did caused the people to wonder, to follow Him (for a while, at least) and to receive healing for themselves and their loved ones. The sad fact, however, is that, except for Mary the mother of Jesus and John, He was alone at the cross.

The manifestations were real enough, and caused people to realize that the Holy Spirit was truly moving in our midst. They cannot, therefore, be discounted, discredited or denied. They were not, however, the only important fruit of the Renewal. The growth of the individual believers and of the groups, the drawing together of all believers in Israel to become one in the Body of Christ, the breaking down of denominational and historical barriers and the building of a deep desire to know ever more about God ... these were all important and unmistakable fruits of the Renewal.

The growth of various groups of believers in Israel during this period brings me to the next subject. I call it "A Tale of Two Congregations."

CHAPTER FIVE

§

A TALE OF TWO CONGREGATIONS

THE ANGLICANS IN ISRAEL HAD HELD SERVICES FOR MANY
years in a large complex of buildings in Joppa which
had been built in the latter part of the nineteenth
century by Baron Ustinov, the grandfather of the
actor Peter Ustinov. Later, the complex had become
a hotel. Then the British organization CMJ (the
Church's Ministry Among the Jews) acquired
ownership of the property — only to have it com-
mandeered, first by the British army in the Second
World War for a military prison, and then by the
Israeli Army in 1948. CMJ was able to regain ownership of the complex in the 1950s. By that time, it
was in a dilapidated condition.

Canon Roger Allison conducted services there for
many years. The small group that attend his services
was, for the most part, made up of middle-aged Jewish believers who had arrived in Israel destitute.
They did not speak Hebrew and had a very difficult time adjusting to Israeli life. Canon Allison
struggled with the tiny group until 1968, when he

was called to Jerusalem to become head of CMJ and vicar of Christ Church.

Rev. and Mrs. Henry Knight arrived in 1967 to take up duties at the Immanuel House (Beit Immanuel), as the establishment in Joppa had come to be called. Henry, a Jewish believer himself, wondered if the conventional Anglican approach was the way to present Christ to the Jewish people, and he was praying that God would show him what to do.

Henry actually felt that his own time could be better utilized in a ministry he considered to be his main calling — a ministry to university students. He began a search for someone else to serve the congregation so that he could be free to fulfill this other calling. Very soon after he arrived, he began a ministry to students at the Tel Aviv University.

Henry communicated his desire for a permanent pastor for Beit Immanuel to Roy Kreider, who was then attending the Baptist Village church. In the congregation, there was a young electronics engineer, a Presbyterian layman by the name of Art Ehrlick. Art had become convinced that the Lord had something more for him to do, and seeking to know what this might be, he had gone off by himself for a period of meditation and prayer. While he sought the Lord, he received a vision in which the Lord revealed to him that he was to pastor a congregation in the Tel Aviv-Joppa area. This seemed very strange to him, since he was a layman, but when he came back from his time of seeking God alone, he shared the vision with the rest of our prayer group, and we began to pray for the fulfillment of that promise.

When Roy learned of Art's vision, he informed Henry, and the three men began to pray for the Lord's leading. Two members of the Immanuel House staff, Janette Ross and Barbara Logsdon, both from Scotland, joined the men in praying for God's will.

Attendance at the church until this time was so low, about twenty-five, that the church had considered selling the existing property. They planned to use the money from the sale to purchase another building in the Tel Aviv area that could serve as a study center and hostel (as well as a place of worship). After a contractor assured them that the foundations of the building were solid and that it could safely be remodeled, they began reconsidering this move. The confirmation came in a dream in which Art saw a dove descending from Heaven and lighting on Immanuel House. This was received as a sign that the Holy Spirit meant for them to retain the present property.

The idea behind the study center was that such small attendance did not warrant the maintenance on such a large building. A study center might attract people from all over the country and perhaps even from overseas. Art's acceptance of responsibility for the services left Henry and Roy free to work on plans for the study center.

As it turned out, Art's ministry with the congregation was of short duration, as he was forced to return to the States the following spring for family reasons. When this happened, Henry asked Roy to take over the services, but Roy, feeling that the study center should be his main objective, suggested Paul and Bertha Swarr, and they accepted.

Paul recalls the early days of his ministry at Immanuel: "As to the condition of the congregation when I took over, let it be said that Art had a wonderful personality and had a warm heart for those who were in trouble. The congregation, however, was made up mostly of Jewish middle-aged people, and older, and they were people with broken lives who had been believers a long time before they came to Israel. There were twenty-five to thirty in the group when we started attending. Because of the remodeling work, we met in Janette Ross's apartment, just a room really. Services were mainly in English, with touches of Hebrew."

"Roy and Art had been leading toward services that would have more meaning to the local people rather than just copying the services from England or America. With this, the congregation had already started growing. Members of the staff, Janette Ross, Barbara Logsdon and the Knights, had started to emphasize the Sunday evening worship because the Sunday morning service was aimed toward the expatriate group. Then, CMJ agreed to allow Rev. Bill Wilson to start a home meeting in the Hertzlia area for expatriates, thus freeing the evening service at Immanuel for local Hebrew-speaking people.

"Young Jewish believers began to come in toward the end of the 1970s. One of the major reasons for the growth, I believe, was the renovation of the building complex. John Relf and a team of volunteers from abroad started the work in the summer of 1977, and the renovations went on for five years, until 1982. When they were finished, the old thirty-three room building had been transformed into a youth hostel and study center, with all new worship facilities.

"Over the years, more than two hundred volunteers came from overseas to help with the work. Mostly young people, they became part of the fellowship, and some of them never left. They were able to influence some local young people, and they too joined the fellowship.

"A big change in the music used in the services contributed to the growth of the congregation. Previously, when we had sung in Hebrew, we had used translated hymns. Now, we began to use choruses from the Bible, usually from the Book of Psalms. We also began to use other musical instruments: guitars, tambourines and drums.

"Then a group of believers began to write original songs in Hebrew. It actually began when a Youth With A Mission group led the congregation in this type of music for a period of eight weeks. People loved this new music, and others continued it after the YWAM team had moved on.

"We began forming home fellowship groups in the autumn of 1981. While everyone continued to come to the weekend meetings, five or six groups (each comprised of ten to twenty members) began to meet once a week in different homes, hosted by young couples. These meetings helped the young people to become more involved in the life of the congregation. They took great pride in having a fellowship meeting in their homes.

"The makeup of the congregation at Beit Immanuel, about half Jewish through the years, remained fairly constant, but by the mid 1980s, attendance at regular worship services had grown to about a hundred members. Visitors sometimes swelled this number considerably. Once, we counted twenty-three different languages being spoken among those present. As more Sabras (native-born Israelis) began to attend, Hebrew became the predominant language. The available space was eventually strained, and we began praying about what to do.

"Many (but not all) of the young Jews coming into the congregation could be termed 'Charismatics,' but the form of worship had now become Charismatic. It was not 'wildly' so, but we did have the gifts of the Spirit manifested in our worship services. We left ourselves open for any eventuality, and the Lord did speak to us through prophetic words of encouragement.

"Once a month, following our Communion service, we invited those with physical needs to come forward to be anointed with oil and prayed for to receive healing. Derek Prince of England came and conducted a seminar on healing. He taught that healing is not always physical. There are also psychological and spiritual healings. Several remarkable healings occurred during the seminar. One person who had suffered from asthma for years was healed.

"On the first weekend of each month, we began having three services — one in English at Beit Immanuel, one in English and Hebrew in Ramat Gan and one in Hebrew at our house. We felt that the Lord wanted us to 'lengthen our stakes' and move out into other locations. In each service, we spent some time in worship and hearing the Word preached, and then we broke up into smaller groups to pray. This was more informal than a church service.

"The attitude of [our] Mennonite Board has been positive. They have been gratified to see the ministry growing and to see the work of God expanded. They have had to deal with similar things happening among our people in other countries, especially France and Belgium." [21]

Another congregation showing phenomenal growth as a result of the Renewal was the Jerusalem Baptist Church located at 4 Narkis Street in Jerusalem. The little chapel, which seated sixty people, was built in 1933, and except for a period during the 1948 War, had hosted continued worship services faithfully. There had been, during all this time, some twenty to twenty-five members in the congregation, and sometimes fewer. Then the Renewal came.

Dr. R.L. Lindsey, pastor of the congregation, relates what happened: "I had an experience with the Holy Spirit while attending a meeting at Stella Carmel in early 1975. Since others of us in Jerusalem were having similar experiences, after I returned to the city, a group of us, made up of men and women from several denominations (including Roman Catholics), began to meet together several times each week just to seek the will of the Lord in our lives. We felt that God was trying to break through in our community and throughout Israel. We met this way for about three years, sensing that God wanted to do great things in our lives — if we would just be open to His working through His power in the Holy Spirit. In our little prayer group, we felt the presence of the Lord powerfully.

"We were still having regular worship services in our little Baptist chapel, just as we had been doing for forty years. We began to feel, however, that God was striving to do something special in our services. We made some changes. For one, we began to sing more choruses. We began to be more free in our worship and tried to follow the flow of the Holy Spirit as we worshipped. We began to praise more, and we began to experience the joy of the Lord in our services.

"By the fall of that year, our congregation had grown to seventy-five, mostly young people, and we began to experience problems with space. We tried having an additional service, this one on Sunday nights, but something seemed to be wrong. Then God revealed to us that there was a real need for forgiveness among us and that we would not be able to find His will for that service until the needed forgiveness was given and received. We began to search our hearts, and when any of us found that he or she was harboring ill feelings toward others, we forgave each other. We were soon able to pray and to receive God's guidance.

"One Sunday night, twelve to fifteen of us were together. We invited anyone who felt the need of prayer to come sit in a chair set in the middle of the circle, and we would lay hands on that person. There was a Jewish fellow there who was suffering from pains in his back. He came forward and sat in the chair, and we laid hands on him and prayed. Later, he told a friend, a Jewish truck driver, 'You ought to go to that Baptist meeting. They sit you in a chair, they lay hands on you and pray for you, and there is an electric charge that goes from your head to your toes, and you feel better.' This was the first time anyone had been healed in our meetings, but it certainly was not the last.

"One Sunday night, a Jewish lady came to one of our services with a stiff neck. She had been told by the doctors that the cause of the stiffness was the deterioration of the cartilage in her neck and that she would just have to live with it. We asked her if there had been any history in her family of someone with extreme anger. She replied that there certainly had been — her grandfather. He would become so filled with rage that his whole body would stiffen like a board and become fiery red. We prayed against any spirit of rebellion that she may have inherited from her grandfather. As we prayed, she slumped to the floor. When she stood up, the stiffness in her neck was gone, and it never returned.

"The congregation grew more, until we could not get all of the people into the little chapel. Some seventy-five crowded in, but that left many others standing outside, looking in through the windows. One of the members suggested that we knock down the walls behind the pulpit which separated the chapel from two class rooms. No sooner had we completed this, however, than this added space was also filled.

"In the spring of 1976, we took out the windows on the east side of the church, put some canvas over the area between the chapel and the Baptist House, and let the people sit under it. After that, we removed everything from within the chapel that we could and covered the entire area with a tin roof. The result was not 'pretty,' but we had to do something; we had two hundred people coming to our services by this time.

"Then in 1982, arsonists burned the chapel to the ground. About the same time, people from all over the world came to attend the annual 'Feast of Tabernacles' in Jerusalem. We took advantage of the presence of Jamie Buckingham in the city and asked him to speak for us on the weekend. We held the service in the open air, with the people standing in the ruins of the chapel. More than six hundred of those who had been attending the Feast of Tabernacles celebration attended our meeting. An offering was taken that day, and more than twelve thousand dollars was collected, nearly as much as our total annual budget until then. That was the beginning of our building fund for a new church building.

"We put up a tent to house the congregation in the meantime, but this proved to be rather unsatisfactory. We then erected a large 'tabernacle' built of metal and plastic, and we worshipped in that until we could secure a building permit for a new church building.

"In 1992, we dedicated our new church building. The cost of it was over a million dollars, and the major part of the funds was raised by the congregation. We now have between three and four hundred people coming each weekend, and for them we have twelve Sabbath school classes. We have three main worship services during the week, two in English and one in Hebrew. Our services continue to be very loosely structured, with much singing and with a great deal of joy. We baptize an average of thirty new people each year. The spiritual life of the church is directed by elders, whom we call *Ro'em* (Hebrew for 'shepherds').

"We have assumed a leadership role in encouraging other groups in the city. The Christ Church congregation has become more free in its worship, and people are crowding to its services. There is a growing congregation of Pentecostals at the Y.M.C.A. each Sunday. All in all, there are five large and active congregations in Jerusalem, and many other small groups. The Holy Spirit is moving in a tremendous way in Jerusalem, and the end is not yet." [22]

As the Holy Spirit's power was being felt in the Jewish and expatriate circles in Israel, He was also

at work among the Arab Christians. We have already seen that many Arab Christians were involved
in bringing in the Renewal. For the most part, Arab
Christians responded across the board with warmth
and enthusiasm to the movement. In the next chapter, I want to demonstrate more fully how the Holy
Spirit manifested Himself in the lives of individual
Arabs.

CHAPTER SIX

§

THE RENEWAL AMONG THE CHRISTIAN ARABS

IN MANY WAYS, THE CHRISTIAN ARABS OF ISRAEL HAD AS much, if not more, to do with bringing the Renewal into the country than did any other group. For example, it was Pastor Fahid Karmout, then pastor of the Jerusalem Baptist Church (East), who was influential in urging the team led by Costa Deir to conduct teaching seminars in Jerusalem. Pastor Karmout had grown up with Costa in Ramle.

The Arab believers in Israel had many wonderful experiences of deliverance from demons as a result of the Renewal. Ray Register, Baptist representative in Nazareth, relates one such experience at which he was present: "I was a witness to a case of demon possession in a little Arab community on the West Bank, close to the city of Jenin. The newspapers had been carrying stories about a family in the little village that was being tormented by demons. Pastor Fahid Karmout took me with him to visit the family. I saw a house that had almost been destroyed on the inside. All the cooking utensils had been shot full of holes. The family's clothes had been cut to shreds.

"The woman of the house had become so terrified that her hair had turned white. A demon had appeared to the young boy in the family. The demon had the head of a goat and the body of a girl.

"This was my first experience with demons, and I was scared out of my wits. Pastor Karmout prayed with the family, binding the demon in the name of Jesus, and the demon must have left because peace returned to the household."[23]

Dr. Ray Pritz, who worked with the Bible Society in Israel and was one of the editors on the Annotated Hebrew New Testament project, described another case of demon possession and its exorcism by an Arab pastor: "Rev. Naim Nasser, pastor of the Bethlehem Lutheran Church, discovered that a young married Arab lady had been possessed by several spirits. He called Pastor Karmout, and the two spent five hours exorcising eight unclean spirits (whose names were revealed when the pastors demanded the demons to identify themselves).

"This experience led to further work with possessed people in Bethlehem and in Beit Jala. It was discovered that a great number of people, Moslems and nominal Christians, had been brought under the control of spirits. Deliverance from these spirits was made possible only through the power of the name of Jesus."

The Renewal continued to spread among the Arab Christians, especially in Nazareth. The Pastor of the Baptist church there, Rev. Fuad Sackhnini, and his deacons began to have experiences with the Holy Spirit. Then revivals began to break out all over the Galilee. The life of Ray Register suddenly took on a new dimension. He wrote: "Lee Bivins called me on November 5, 1971, to tell me that my mother had died. I shared my grief with the pastor, Rev. Fuad Sackhnini, and he suggested that we drive down to the Immanuel House in Joppa where Costa Deir was speaking. When I told Costa about my mother dying, he revealed to me that God had given him a vision in which He had expressed His love for me and said that He was going to use me as a key person in the Galilee. As Costa was speaking, a great pressure erupted from me in praise to God.

"The next morning, the same praise came from deep inside of me. I prayed for power to witness to the Moslems. That very same day, in the morning, I was given the opportunity to witness to a professor at the University of Haifa. He was a Moslem. In the afternoon, I was given the opportunity to meet a former Communist youth leader in Nazareth. He took me to the Arab villages and introduced me to the sheiks, who all knew him. In the days ahead (through reading the Koran in Arabic along with the Bible), I was able to discover a whole new pattern of thought for witnessing to Moslems.

"People began to believe and to come to me to be baptized. I took a picture of one man whom I baptized, and was surprised to see in the developed photo a shaft of light above his head. There was also a dove in the picture.

"In October of 1973, the Yom Kippur War broke out. There had been services in Rama, and there had been a week-long meeting in Nazareth, but nothing had happened. On Friday night, we met in the home of Pastor Fuad Sackhnini. There was a girl in the meeting who was demon possessed. She spoke with the voice of a Moslem sheik. This girl had insulted a sheik, and he had placed a spell on her. She was relieved of the demon through the name of Jesus in the meeting that day, and immediately true revival broke out in the house. We all fell on our faces before God. Later, the revival spread to the Nazareth Baptist Church. We had sixty baptisms in one month in the Sea of Galilee during the 1973 War." [24]

George Laty, an Arab deacon in the Nazareth Baptist Church and sixth- and eighth-grade teacher in the Nazareth Baptist School, told of the movement of the Holy Spirit in that school: "During the summer of 1972, Rev. Bahjat Batarsi came to the Nazareth Baptist School to speak on the Holy Spirit. The students were very interested in what he had to say, and after the chapel program, when we returned to class, the sixth graders wanted to hear more about the Holy Spirit.

"As I began to talk, we felt His presence. Then suddenly, one after another of the students began to speak in tongues. I spoke in tongues also, and this was only the second time I had done so. One of the students who understood the Indian language said that I was speaking in a language of India.

"Then suddenly, one of the students cried, ' I see Jesus. He is wearing a crown, and He is placing crowns on all our heads.' Then he cried, 'Don't you see Him? He is standing right by you.' I did not see Jesus, but one after another of the students did. I do not doubt that He was in that room. We prayed for about five minutes more, and then the bell rang for the next class, my eighth grade.

"In this class also, the students asked to hear more about the Holy Spirit. As I was speaking, the same thing happened. One of the students cried, 'I see Jesus. He is wearing a crown and carrying His cross.' Although I did not see Jesus myself, there is no doubt in my mind that the students did.

"These students come from many backgrounds: Roman Catholic, Greek Orthodox and even Moslem. I was trying to share a verse of scripture with them to explain what was happening, but I couldn't think of the verse I wanted to use. Then one of the students said, 'Teacher, look at Acts 2:17.' It was the very verse I had been thinking of. It said this:

" 'In the last days, God says, I will pour out my Spirit on all people. Your sons and daughters will prophesy, your young men will see visions, your old men will dream dreams.'

"These students came later to church and related what had happened that day in the classroom. Their parents began to call me and ask what was going on. Sixteen of those students continued to speak in tongues, and the message was always the same: 'I am with you, My little sheep. Be encouraged and not discouraged. I am coming soon. Stick close to the Word of God.'

"There has been much growth in the spiritual lives of both the teachers and the students because of that visitation by Jesus. Priests of several denominations came to me, wanting to hear about what had happened in those classrooms. Now, we have about fifty young people who meet each Saturday to pray and to worship God." [25]

Dr. Robert Lindsey accompanied Fahid Karmout (at the pastor's request) as he was engaged in dealing with a case of demon possession in an Arab woman. The demon was rejecting the pastor's attempts to exorcise it by screaming in the Hebrew language. Pastor Kamout, being Arab, spoke little Hebrew, so when it happened again, Lindsey took over.

He later told what happened: "I spoke to the spirits in Hebrew, and the woman became very agitated. The spirits began to speak in some strange language that sounded like Chinese. I became very angry and wished more than anything to be able to speak whatever language the spirits were speaking so that I could confront them. I opened my mouth and said two or three words of mere mumbling. Then, suddenly, I became fluent in that language.

"Then the spirits really began to shout, and I began to shout right back at them. We had a real shouting match. Pastor Karmout thought for a moment that the demon had gotten into me, as it had the woman. He began to sing a hymn, and the woman quieted down. This experience was the beginning of my ministry in the Holy Spirit." [26]

Two tragic tests of our faith were soon to confront the believing community. In 1972, Samuel Laty, the son of George and Antoinette Laty (both teachers in the Baptist School in Nazareth), developed leukemia. The Latys were among the finest and best-loved of the Christian community in Israel.

There was a Christmas offering taken every year among Baptists called the Lottie Moon Christmas Offering. It was named for the first Baptist missionary to China. George Laty was such an enthusiastic promoter of that offering that it was jokingly referred to in Israel as the "Laty Moon" Christmas Offering. George and his wife were such earnest soul winners for the Lord that he was invited repeatedly to speak in churches in the United States.

Samuel was the Latys' only son (there was also a married daughter). He was so spiritually mature for his sixteen years that he, too, was invited to the States to speak. It was on such a tour that his disease was discovered.

A son is so important to an Arab family that it is the custom, when the first son is born, for the father to change his own name to that of his son. George, according to the practice, became "Abu Samuel" (father of Samuel). The thought of losing their son was unbearable to the Laty family.

Upon hearing of Samuel's illness, the believers in Israel immediately mounted a prayer campaign for his healing. Healing miracles had become commonplace by then. The attitude of the believers was, "We have prayed, so of course God will heal Samuel." But it didn't happen. Samuel became so ill that he was rushed back to Israel, and he died within days of his return.

The believing community was rocked by this tragedy. It was the first major defeat of the Renewal, and suddenly, confidence was replaced by confusion.

What had gone wrong? In an attempt to understand, another serious error was made. Some tactless persons went to the grieving parents and suggested that they had caused the death of their own son by concealing sin in their lives. This action (by these Job's comforters) so enraged me that I proceeded to write an editorial for the publication *Hayahad Digest*, which I edited at the time. An excerpt from that editorial appears below.

The Latys, though rendered prostrate by their grief, lived through this tragedy and returned to their spiritual leadership roles with an added dimension of their faith, which was an inspiration to us all. Those visiting the Latys for the purpose of consoling the grieving family were comforted themselves by George and Antoinette's quiet acceptance of the Lord's will.

The second shock to the believers also occurred in the Arab community. This incident, too, was mentioned in my editorial: "In 1948, many Arab children were left behind when their parents fled because of the War. Some of the children were orphans; others could not be supported by their families. The Baptists began, in 1948, a home for nineteen of these children and called it the George W. Truett Home after a famous Baptist preacher in Texas. In 1955, the home was moved to what is now the Baptist Village, near Petach Tikva.

"One of these children was named Milady. Born on Christmas Day, her name meant 'Christmas' in Arabic. Milady grew up in the home at Baptist Village, and then she married Eliya Qubty, a deacon in the Nazareth Baptist Church and a teacher in the Nazareth Baptist School. As time went on, three children were born to the couple. Then, in 1974, Milady contracted leukemia.

"Again the believers mounted a war of prayer against the disease. Long vigils of all-night prayer were held throughout the country. Many fasted. Milady was anointed with oil; hands were laid on her in prayer, and the same optimistic claims for the certainty of her recovery were made. Had not Jesus promised, 'If two or more ask anything in my Name, they shall receive it'? Wasn't the same Lord who healed when He walked the earth still able to answer His children's pleas today?

"But Milady continued to decline and had to be admitted to the hospital. On Good Friday, March 28, 1975, someone passing Milady's room heard her singing, 'He lives, He lives, Christ Jesus lives today.' Later that night, Milady died, and once again, the believers had to agonize before the Lord with the question of 'why?'

"Gratefully, this time, there were no efforts to place blame; there was only the grief that ravished our hearts. The usual platitudes were offered: 'She is better off,' 'She is in a better place,' etc., but such statements have always rankled my soul. They may be true enough (they certainly were in Milady's case), but the sight of a grieving husband and three little children left motherless brought a taste of bitterness to my heart. No truism could explain that which was inexplicable.

"Although the community was unable to prevent the tragedy, it did attempt to ease the pain of it with love and empathy. No people can show more concern than an Arab community, and those who stepped in to help in this case included a major part of the Christians in Nazareth. This writer can be forgiven, perhaps, a sense of pride in the fact that his daughter moved into the Qubty home to take care of the family for several months.

"Shortly afterwards, Elia married Rhadia, another of the 'home kids,' a wonderful Christian, and the grief of loss was turned to rejoicing throughout the land.

"What did God teach us through these lessons in pain? He taught us that He is sovereign and that He has no less love for us when, in His sovereign will, He chooses *not* to answer every prayer in the way we would wish. He taught us that it is futile to look for scapegoats when things go wrong. Certainly it is folly to mix the gall of blame with the vinegar of pain.

"I personally gained great comfort from this truth. This is not to say that I did not grieve for the Latys and for Elia and his children. They were my dear friends, and I agonized with and for them. What comforted me was the knowledge that God is sovereign and that He controls the past, the present and the future. He is not the chairman of some board, depending on the decisions others make. He is also not some waiter with a towel draped over His arm, waiting attentively for our every command.

"This is certainly not fatalism, nor is it determinism. I do expect answers to my prayers, and I receive them. I do believe that prayer changes things; if it didn't, why would we even bother to pray? At the same time, however, God sometimes chooses (in His wisdom) to deny my request, and He is not compelled to give me a reason. He sovereignly acts, and He expects me to realize that He loves me — whether He grants a particular prayer or not. And I do.

"God is on His throne; He is in command; the future is in His hands, and the universe does not turn on the axis of my frailty. In this truth, there is rest.

"From time to time, as men beseech God to heal, either themselves or their loved ones, winds of hope blow as the Holy Spirit grants miracles of healing. Man has always longed for 'a state of grace' in which sickness would become a thing of the past, where prayer would activate the power of God, transcending the need for medicine or doctors. A sizable portion of the New Testament is taken up with describing the healing miracles of Christ and His disciples. As far as that goes, don't we look back, almost in awe, at the old country doctor who healed with love and common sense and very little else?

"What is divine healing and how does it differ from psychosomatic medicine, of which psychology is so familiar, or the autosuggestion of the professional counselor? Is the mind able to heal the body on signal from a suggestion by a person with the charismatic power to induce in that patient a 'labor of faith'? Many psychiatrists would answer, 'Certainly.' The point is that this sort of healing occurs every day; it happens to those who aren't Christians, who are being treated by persons who are not Christians and with methods which have nothing to do with divine healing.

"We are talking about the instances when God transcends space and time to grant a miracle of healing in response to prayer. Do such miracles happen? Of course they do. It would be a rare thing to encounter a serious Christian who has not experienced some such miracle of divine healing — either in his own life or in the life of a loved one.

"In James 5:14, the 'elders' of which James spoke were, I would gather, just simple believers in Jesus.

They were devoted to Christ, to be sure. They were set aside by the congregation for their purity of life, to be sure. Yet they were still just plain people. James ascribed the ministry of healing to a group of believers who, in obedience to the Word of God, simply beseech God for His healing. This act is beautiful in its simplicity and utterly devoid of self-glorification.

"The teaching is sometimes heard that the healing depends on a person's faith or the faith of the loved ones praying for healing. If there is no healing, then the faith was at fault. If the prayers had been sincere or not rendered ineffective by sin, there would have been healing. This teaching is more often implied than expressed, but the meaning is discernible, and it has often had a devastating effect on grieving loved ones.

"For a family in shock over the loss of a loved one to be told that they are guilty of causing the death because of their lack of faith saddles them with guilt, forsakes empathy and borders on the sadistic.

"No! While divine healing is certainly a reality and is certainly to be sought after in the life of the believer, let it never be taught that healing lies anywhere except in the hands of a sovereign God who heals as He wills. Let it be stated that sometimes God chooses (for His own purposes) that healing, at least the particular healing that has been prayed for, is *not* granted. Let it be stressed that healing is according to the dictates of an all-powerful God and that man shares neither in the glory (if there is healing) or in the guilt (if there is not)."

Thus, we, as a believing community, learned the lessons of the Renewal. *Line upon line, precept upon precept,* we matured toward God's presence.

The Renewal was not limited, in any sense of the word, to the Protestant believers. Roman Catholic believers in Israel also felt His power during this time.

Chapter Seven

§

The Renewal in the Roman Catholic Community

THE RENEWAL IN THE ROMAN CATHOLIC community began in Jerusalem. Rev. Lawrence Tiller [27] traced its development: "The movement [28] as such among local Catholics can be traced back to a short week-end conference at Stella Carmel near Haifa in February 1971. Some thirty-five Catholics from Tel Aviv and Jerusalem, seeking to strengthen their faith and make their worship more meaningful, gathered to pray together and to share experiences. This conference led to the formation of a nucleus of believers who began weekly prayer and discussion groups, meeting in the Zion House of the American Pentecostal Mission in Jerusalem, under the leadership of Rev. Charles Kopp.

"The highlight of these meetings was the Communion service. In it, the participants were led to praise God in spontaneous singing, which seemed to transport them right up to the throne of God.

"In the group, there were those who had already been baptized in the Holy Spirit and others who requested the laying on of hands and the receiving of the baptism of the Spirit.

"In June 1971, ninety people from all over Israel gathered in Jerusalem to hear Rev. Michael Harper. He stressed the fact that God was leading believers across denominational lines so as to bind them together in this movement of the Holy Spirit. In this way, He would renew His Church.

"In May 1972, more than a hundred leaders of virtually every denomination represented in Israel (including Roman Catholics, as well as Jewish and Arab believers) met for a conference in Jerusalem to hold a truly ecumenical prayer service. It was against the background of this prayer service and others that followed that the Roman Catholic Prayer Group emerged.

"It was while the Roman Catholics were seeking the Lord's leading that Brother Jim Hansom arrived to begin a year's research at the Ecumenical Institute at Tantur, near Bethlehem. Almost simultaneously with the arrival of Brother Hansom, Father Terence Keegan, O.P., arrived at the École Biblique in Jerusalem. These two leaders were instrumental in teaching the Roman Catholic community in the things of the Spirit.

"Mrs. Lawrence Tiller, a Pentecostal, was instrumental in starting a Roman Catholic prayer group.

She, with the help of a nun, Sister Marie Goldstein, initiated a group which included six Benedictine monks, a priest, three nuns and seven Roman Catholic laypeople. Mrs. Tiller remembers this first meeting, in December of 1972, as one of great joy and peace in which the presence of God was awe-inspiring.

"In October 1973, Rev. Francis Martin arrived at the École Biblique and began to lead the group. Under his leadership, the group was led to pray for the leaders of the thirty-eight separate Christian denominations represented in Israel. They were led to realize how the past history of hostility between Christians was breaking the heart of Christ.

"This was an English-speaking group, but several French-speaking Catholics attended the meetings to observe how the group was organized. Their desire was to begin a group of their own.

"In 1973, a French-speaking prayer service was begun in Jerusalem, with four sisters from France ministering to the group. These nuns had been active in a similar movement of the Holy Spirit in France. The importance of this French-speaking prayer group is obvious when it is realized that eighty percent of the Roman Catholics in Jerusalem were French-speaking.

"There was no city in the world where the divisions among Christians were as manifest as in

Jerusalem. Besides the thirty-eight different denominations represented in the country, there were many nondenominational groups, and these often had no fellowship with other believers. The Roman Catholics, the Greek Orthodox, the Coptics, the Greek Catholics, the Jewish believers and the Arab believers were all from different lifestyles and mindsets, and this had created a spiritual Tower of Babel. No greater hope had existed, in modern times, than for the healing of these great wounds in the Body of Christ. This began to happen through the Renewal brought by the work of the Holy Spirit." [29]

Music was an ever-present part of the Renewal. The following chapter describes its contribution.

Chapter Eight

※

The Music and the Worship

of the Renewal

Two elements characterized the Renewal above all others — the music and the worship — and the two of them were so intertwined that they are difficult to separate. The music of the Renewal was designed around praise; it was the music of worship. The preaching of the Renewal was often more teaching than exhortation, and although it was always an integral part of the service, it tended to be overshadowed by the worship.

The music of the Renewal can be classified into two main parts: that which was brought into Israel from other countries, and that which was produced by the local believers. The choruses from overseas tended to be short, simple and joyful tunes, usually based on scripture. The Book of Psalms was a favorite source of the texts. These choruses served the Renewal well, as there were no songbooks available which contained hymns that were familiar to everyone. (We had come from such varied backgrounds.) We needed music that could be learned quickly and easily.

Some choruses quickly became favorites and were sung at most every gathering. Among them were: "There's a Sweet, Sweet Spirit in This Place," "Jesus, Jesus, Jesus," "We Are One in the Spirit," "Holy Spirit, Heavenly Dove" and "Hallelujah." There were at least sixty others. One chorus, "This Is the Day" (from Psalm 118:24), became virtually the theme song of the Renewal and was often used to open the worship services.

Printing these choruses in Hebrew and Arabic, as well as English, solved the language problem and allowed everyone to join in the singing. The singing at services went on for extended periods, often an hour or longer. Even those who grumbled at the length of the services would testify to the blessings received through the worship.

These choruses, however, were not the music of the land, just as the European and American Christian hymns, which had been translated into Hebrew, had not been. In 1956, a hymnal, *Sheer Hadash* (*A New Song*), the work of Robert Lindsey and Miss Ruth Laurence, had been produced by translating familiar Christian hymns such as "The Old Rugged Cross," "Amazing Grace" and "Rock of Ages." In 1976, another collection of hymns, *Hallel Vah Zimrot*

Yah (Praise and Songs to God), the work of Victor Smadja, a Jewish believer and manager of Yanetz Press in Jerusalem was produced. This hymnal was so widely used that it came to be known as "the brown book" because of the color of its cover. It differed from *Sheer Hadash* in that it contained several songs written by local believers.

In 1972, Peter Van Woerden, custodian of the Garden Tomb in Jerusalem, wrote several original Hebrew songs, and Robert Lindsey has continually, through the years, written choruses in Hebrew — mostly for the benefit of the Jerusalem Baptist Church congregation.

Then, in 1977, David and Lisa Loden, professional musicians, composed fifteen original songs in Hebrew and bound them together into *Roni Bat Zion (Rejoice, Daughter of Zion)*. The local fellowships, hungry for music with an Israeli flavor, immediately began singing these songs in their services.

In 1980, Kelvin and Nancy Sebastian, also professional musicians, produced "Bo Lifanav" ("Come Before Him"), "Sos Asis" ("I Will Rejoice") and "Hallelujah." The total of the original songs in Hebrew written by the Lodens and the Sebastians was over seventy and made up the new "hymnals" of the Renewal.

David does not think that the texts of the music written for believers in Israel will ever follow the direction of the hymns of Christian churches in other countries. In Israel, the Scriptures will remain the most important source for the texts of worship songs.

David served as conductor of the "Singers of Praise" choir, which had its roots with the nineteen Arab children raised at the Baptist Village. In the 1950s, Milton and Marty Murphey, Baptist representatives, were in charge of the village. Marty began the choir for the sake of the children.

Later, as expatriates expressed an interest in singing, Marty formed the "Protestant Community Choir" which, for years, sang Handel's *Messiah* every Christmas and Easter. The choir, with an ensemble from the Israeli Philharmonic Orchestra, won praise from the Israeli public. The Murpheys had the complete text of *Messiah* printed in Hebrew and Arabic (as well as English), and this was most effective. (*Messiah* has been called "the fifth Gospel.")

When the Murpheys retired, the name of the choir was changed to "Singers of Praise." David Loden, as director, widened the choir's repertoire and increased the numbers of concerts.

Kelvin and Nancy Sebastian, who wrote the lion's share of the great four-part collection of songs used in the Renewal, were members of the Baptist fellowship in Jerusalem. Kelvin expressed some thoughts concerning the music of the Renewal: " 'Sing unto the Lord a new song!' How many times do we read this command in the Word of God, exhorting us not to forget to fulfill a role in our fellowship with the Father which should be enjoyable, even exciting? Yet so often we are satisfied with the old wine, rather than allowing the Holy Spirit to fill us each day to the point of overflowing. It is from this overflow that we receive that 'new song.' When we do permit ourselves to enter into God's plan of revival, we very naturally open our hearts and our mouths and pour forth the glory and honor and blessing due Him. According to rabbinic tradition, the 'new song' will be written only when the Messiah returns. Well, He has already come."

Kelvin stated that in writing Christian music, the melody should always serve the words, making it easy for the hearer to understand both the text and the script of the song. He added: "The Israelis love music, especially folk music. This means that the believer can write in a style which is both beautiful and innocent and still be accepted. What a relief not to have to incorporate 'rock-and-roll' beats in order to be accepted."

Kelvin related how a former hippie, whose mind had been almost destroyed by drugs, met the Lord and was gloriously saved. This salvation experience restored his mind, and he praised God in song with these words: *"Behold, as the eyes of servants look unto the hand of their masters, and as the eyes of a maiden unto the hand of her mistress so our eyes wait upon the LORD our God, until that he have mercy upon us"* (Psalm 123).

Israeli music is described by Kelvin as being made up of Eastern melodies put together with Western harmonies. All modern instruments have been played according to Western harmony since the time of Bach. Thus, Eastern melodies differ from the West. The basis of a Western melody, for instance, is the fifth of, say "C" to "F," while the basis of Eastern melodies is the *fourth* of "C" to "F." This means that where the Western melodies jump back and forth in fifths, Eastern melodies jump back and forth in fourths, creating a very different type of sound than that with which many Westerners are familiar.

In addition, according to Kelvin, there are, in Eastern music, what might be called "embellishments," which are decorative movements that are quite different from those found in Western music. There is such a thing as "identifiable Israeli music," which fits into definite patterns. Most of the music which is now know as "Messianic music" in the West is not Israeli music at all; it is Hasidic. Even though this music has a particular sound, mainly because of the use of the clarinet and the accordion, a close analysis of the harmony and melody will disclose a Western flavor.

Kelvin discussed at some length the music of the First and Second Temple periods (the times of Solomon

and of Herod): "We do not know what the music
sounded like back then, but we do know the instruments that were used. They were mostly percussion
instruments, like the tambourine and the drum, and
string instruments having only one string. There is
mention in the Book of Psalms of a ten-stringed harp,
but even it, musicologists agree, was monotonic.
There was nothing like what we now know as harmony until well into the second or third century AD.

"Even today, in Orthodox Jewish circles, although
there is much singing, it is more like chanting
(*hazanoot*) than the singing of hymns in Christian
churches. There are no musical instruments in Orthodox synagogues on the Sabbath or on holidays.
The absence of musical instruments is a sign of
mourning for the destruction of the Temple in 70 AD.

"Orthodox Jewish music tends to be sad. This is
not true of secular Israeli music, where there is much
joy and dancing. In this respect, the music of the
Renewal is nearer to Israeli secular music than to
the religious Jewish music. This does not hold true,
of course, for the ontent, but only for the mode of
expression." [30]

David Loden stated that the music of the Renewal
traces back to the praise and joy of the Tabernacle
of David, [31] rather than to the more formal worship
that developed later in the Temple. Again, music of
the the Tabernacle of David differed from that of

the Tabernacle of Moses. David stressed that the music of the Renewal was marked more by simple and joyful choruses than by the solemn and often breathtakingly beautiful requiems of a Verdi or a Mozart or by the soaring cantatas of a Handel or a Steiner.

Kelvin Sebastian agreed, and he added that the reason this was true was that the Renewal was primarily a movement among the young, and few of these young people had the experience to produce more complicated music. This was a positive, rather than a negative, factor. The reason is that as groups from different backgrounds met together, often in countries other than their own, the simple, well-known choruses served to unite rather than divide them.

The Worship [32]

In a remarkable way, the manner of worship in most all of the fellowships caught up in the Renewal varied little. Groups of believers gathered together, and there was a great deal of laughing, hugging and squealing for the joy of being together. The gathering was informal to the extreme, with casual dress and no set order of service. The phrase that comes to mind to describe these gatherings is: "Feel free, and enjoy yourself."

A chorus, such as "Hine Yeshua" ("Here Is Jesus")

or "This Is the Day," served to bring the people to their seats and start the singing. Almost immediately, the congregation would stand and remain standing throughout most of the praise service, which usually went on for an hour or more. There was much clapping and lusty singing. The words for the choruses were usually supplied by an overhead projector.

The musical instrument of choice for these occasions was the guitar. If a piano was present, it might be used, but the guitar was ever-present.

There was a raising of the worshippers' hands in praise, although there was no pressure put on those who felt uncomfortable doing this.

Very often in the larger mass meetings, but less often in the smaller worship services, there occurred a phenomenon commonly called "singing in the Spirit." Someone would begin singing softly in tongues, then another took it up and another ... until the sound rose to a crescendo. Then, slowly, the singing would decrease in volume until it died. This was an uncommonly beautiful experience, and was directed by no one but the Spirit Himself.

On rare occasions, "dancing in the Spirit" also occurred. Other than spontaneous movements by someone expressing joy during a spiritual highpoint in the service, these tended to be disciplined pre-

sentations of biblical texts put to music and interpreted in dance. Psalms 23, 100 and 122 seemed to
lend themselves well to this mode of praise, and I
saw all three beautifully portrayed in dance.

The organization, Youth With A Mission (YWAM),
developed a ministry of dance which was quite suc-
cessful. One of their presentations, "The Toy
Maker," related the creation, the fall of man and the
Passion story and attained such excellence that it
approached the right to be considered a classic. It is
my belief that, along with drama, sacred dance will
begin to be stressed more in the traditional churches
in the future. This is such a natural and joyous expression of delight in the Lord.

One element of Renewal worship often tended to
be a trial to Western-oriented minds. It was the ten-
dency for worshippers to stand for long periods,
perhaps an hour at a time — or even more. As with
the raising of the hands, this practice often caused
those unaccustomed to this style of worship to feel
some embarrassment at being "out of step" with the
others in the congregation. Assurance was often offered in every gathering that both of these reactions
were purely optional and that everyone should feel
free to worship in the way he or she found most
meaningful.

Kelvin Sebastian, for one, felt strongly that it was
important for worshippers to stand. He wrote: "In

any worship, I think that it is important to stand. It is a sign of respect to the Lord. In the Bible, there were really only two positions for worship — standing or lying flat on your face. The word for 'worship' in Hebrew really means 'to prostrate yourself.' In the history of the Church, it was not until after the Reformation that pews and chairs came into use in the churches. You might say that it is more or less a modern idea to worship sitting down."

He had one further word to add to his thoughts on the music of the Renewal: "In music, the rhythm is the least important, but there should be a balance between the harmony, the melody and the rhythm. In 'rock-and-roll' music, the beat takes over everything. The danger in 'Christian rock and roll' is that the people will not even understand the words. There has to be a place in Christian music for a beat; otherwise, you couldn't use drums and cymbals, but the emphasis must be on understanding the words.

"If you come out of a Christian service thumping the beat and not having received the message of the words, something is wrong. The same holds for 'Christian jazz' and even for Christian classical music. Anything that is based on the world is not pleasing to God. The reason that I emphasize the 'new song' so strongly is not because of the songs themselves, but in order to stress the necessity of glorying God. Music must have as its basis the emphasizing of the Word of God.

"Music can be compared to the incense offered up to God in the Tabernacle. Incense was made up of three elements beaten together. Music should be like that. The three parts are melody, harmony and rhythm. Beaten together, they form a 'sweet savor unto the Lord.' "

It might be well to add one more thought concerning the mode of worship in the congregations caught up in the Renewal. It may be that many of these practices will slowly pass away. For my part, I hope that this is not true. It seems to me that the urge to praise God should be the dominant consideration in worship, and it is a sad thing, I think, when we are critical of the unfamiliar.

In the worship of those caught up in the Renewal, there may have been a few — a very tiny few — whose antics were suspect. But so what? The vast majority were sincere in their praise to the Lord. The devotee who is attempting to worship God in a spiritually frozen ecclesiastical setting would do well to warm his heart and soul in one of the boisterous, joyful meetings described above.

Worship, which had begun in the Renewal in small groups, continued in increasingly larger congregations, until it reached the mass proportions described in the following chapter.

Chapter Nine

§

The Mass Meetings

As the Renewal spread, many individual groups began to have larger and larger meetings, culminating in the "World Conference on the Holy Spirit" held in Jerusalem, March 2-5, 1973.

This first mass meeting, sponsored by Logos International Fellowship, Inc., headed by Dan Malechuck, was held in the Binyane Haouma (National Hall), the largest auditorium in Israel. It was attended by four thousand pilgrims from overseas, plus five hundred local believers. Logos International, at enormous expense, paid for the hotel rooms and meals of any of the local believers who attended.

The program began each day at 9:00 AM and continued on late into the night with a list of speakers that read like a "Who's Who" of the Charismatic Movement. Jamie Buckingham (a Baptist pastor from Florida) was the worship and praise leader for the conference. Charles Simpson (another Baptist from Florida) brought messages filled with humor.

The theme of his messages was "The Oneness of the Body of Christ."

Perhaps the highlight of the giant conference was the night that Kathryn Kuhlman conducted her "Miracle Service." Some three hundred persons claimed to have either been healed or helped during that one service. So great was the attendance in the hall that night that TV cameras had to beam the proceedings into three overflow rooms. Afterward, Miss Kuhlman was prevailed upon to have a second "Miracle Service" on the last evening of the conference.

The tone of the conference was quite Charismatic, with the gifts of prophecy, tongues and healing very much in evidence. The manifestations were in no way objectionable. The atmosphere was filled with the presence of the Lord. One came away from it, perhaps not having a perfect understanding of all that had gone on, but nonetheless having the feeling that there had been a "rightness" about it all. There was certainly great joy felt and expressed by those attending.

One puzzling instance occurred when Miss Kuhlman invited to the stage all those who were active in the local ministry. I did not go up, but many, perhaps a hundred, did. Among those who went to the stage was a Jewish Christian pastor of the congregation I attended at Baptist Village. We were very close friends, and I admired him greatly. He had held an important position in the government prior to his acceptance of Christ as Savior. His spiritual change had cost him his position and his family, yet he had remained faithful.

As my friend stood in line on the stage with the others, Miss Kuhlman walked past them and touched each one lightly. At her touch, each one of them fell to the floor and lay there — including my friend. As this was happening, some in the audience, including a Filipino woman sitting next to me, also fell to the floor. Miss Kuhlman explained that this was being "slain in the Spirit." Later, when I discussed this with my friend, he was surprised and could not remember such a thing having happened to him. He was amazed when I told him I had seen him slump to the floor. I must confess that I have never understood this phenomenon.

Following the conference, a three-day seminar was held on "The Gifts of the Spirit." The main emphasis of the teaching was on tongues, interpretation of tongues and prophecy. This seminar was very well attended by local believers.

In November of that following year (1974), the second World Conference on the Holy Spirit was even larger than the first. It drew more than five thousand Christians from overseas and was attended by as many as a thousand local believers. Once again, the tone was joyous.

There was one particular addition to what had transpired in the first conference. It was "singing in the Spirit," and it happened just as I have described it in the chapter on the music and worship of the Renewal. It started very quietly in one section of the building and spread over the whole until it reached a great crescendo. Then, it slowly subsided. Anyone experiencing this marvelous expression of joy and praise would have been blessed, and I certainly was.

Mass meetings continue today, although they are held now under the supervision of the Christian Embassy in Jerusalem and are called "The Festival of Praise."

I hesitate to give to the mass meetings a central place in the Renewal. They served a purpose, especially at the beginning of the Renewal, yet they always retained a foreign tone. In my opinion, their influence was not lasting. The local Jewish believers never attended the giant meetings in great numbers. The 1985 festival did have a feature which was quite interesting. There are many artists among the local Jewish believers, and during this festival, an exhibition of their works was held.

There are large meetings of the Jewish believers which are completely indigenous. These are held during the great holidays: Passover, Succoth, Shavuot (Passover) and Hanukkah. These meetings are conducted by the local believers and have a distinctly Israeli flavor. The meetings have grown steadily and are straining facilities, such as the Baptist Village near Petach Tikva, which can accommodate them.

Such meetings of the local believers are in my opinion, much more exciting and meaningful than a conference, massive though it might be, imported from outside the country.

Mention has already been made of the Renewal being a movement mainly of young people. The next chapter will describe the work of the Holy Spirit among the very young.

CHAPTER TEN

❧

THE YOUNG FACE OF THE RENEWAL

THE RENEWAL, BY AND LARGE, WAS A YOUTH MOVEMENT. A great percentage of those who were blessed by it were under the age of thirty. This is not to say that there were not older believers who were blessed by the Renewal. I have already mentioned some who were. The fact is, however, that a large number of young people came to know the Lord through the Renewal. It was, consequently, the young who set the worship style.

One unique example of activity among the young occurred at the AIS (American International School) in Kfar Shariyahu near Tel Aviv. The majority of the young people attending the school were the children of expatriates, mainly embassy personnel. In the early 1970s, the teenage children of the families caught up in the Renewal began to become active. They held prayer meetings during their recess periods, in which they prayed, sang and worshipped the Lord, and they had their own experiences with the Holy Spirit. The fact that those who were involved in this movement were leaders in every area of AIS life — sports, academics and every other area of school activity — they were able to heavily influence their classmates.

One of the teachers at the school, remarking about these students, stated: "They have set such an example of clean, wholesome living in this school that they have made my task of disciplining immeasurably easier."

Also attending AIS were a number of Israeli children whose parents wanted them to learn to speak English. One of these students, a girl, whom we shall call "Yonah" (*Yonah*, in Hebrew, means "dove"), came from a very wealthy, influential and politically powerful family. Yonah, at first antagonistic toward her Christian classmates, became drawn into discussions with them concerning their faith. These discussions resulted in Yonah examining her own religious beliefs, or lack of them (atheism, agnosticism and impatience with all religions are rampant among Israeli young people).

Yonah was attracted by the joyfulness of these Christian classmates, and she soon became convinced of the validity of their faith. The influence of her new friends began to be reflected in her own life. She brought glowing reports to her friends of her new happiness in her home life. She told of how her parents expressed wonder at the way she had become a person "much easier to live with." Her studies improved also. Her whole life, even to her facial expressions, took on a new and exciting vitality. Yonah's parents were delighted.

This delight came to an abrupt halt when they discovered the reason for Yonah's change. Concerned, more than angry at first, they demanded that Yonah discontinue fellowship with her Christian friends. Her attendance at their meetings was forbidden, and she was subjected to endless lectures from her sister, her parents and other acquaintances as to the evil of "the Mission."

Yonah eventually was forced to leave home. Because of the prominence of the family, the incident received wide coverage in the local press. One newspaper claimed that Yonah had been "filled with demons by the Baptists." Her father took the case to court, but since his daughter had not been witnessed to by missionaries but only by her own classmates, nothing came of it.

Yonah's father then took his case to the Israeli Knesset, demanding that the Baptists be expelled from the country. The case was debated in the Knesset, but, again, because there was no evidence of missionary activity, nothing came of it.

Yonah, through it all, kept a sweet spirit and remained strong in her new faith. After several years, she finally won her place back into her home and into the hearts of her parents. Today, she lives in

Richmond, Virginia, and is married to another Jewish believer. They both are active in the Jewish-Christian fellowship there.

One of the students at AIS at the time, recalled the effect of the Renewal among his classmates: "The kids were full of the joy of the Lord, and we would look forward eagerly to the two recesses every day. When they came, we would go to an empty classroom and meet together for Bible reading, prayer and singing. One of the guys brought a guitar every day to school. When we were forbidden to meet in a classroom, we went out to the football field and had our prayer meeting there.

"Just reading the Bible out loud to the group was fantastic. We couldn't get enough of it. We would just read and sing, and the presence of the Lord became very real. In spite of the fact that the majority of the students around us were Jewish, we were filled with a boldness. There was no fear whatsoever as we worshipped and praised the Lord.

"Those people that did come to know the Lord, like Yonah, did so, not because we were able to explain our faith in such an articulate way or that we were able to answer all their questions. It was simply that they saw the joy of the Lord, and they wanted it.

"I recall going to parties, and while people were dancing, I sat on the couch and sang songs like 'This Is the Day.' I just couldn't help it. I was so full of the

Lord that praises came out all the time. People would come over and ask, 'What are you singing?' and I would reply, 'I am singing to the Lord.' They would ask, 'What is this all about?' Then I would tell them. They had been drawn first, however, by the joy of the Lord.

"What happened at AIS was the sovereign work of the Lord. The presence of the Lord was so strong that it was difficult to think of anything else. One student's testimony was so powerful that he was urged to have it printed. He did, and then he distributed it all over the school, including to the faculty members. One of the teachers, a Jew and a Harvard graduate, was quite touched by this testimony of how the Lord had rescued the student from the drug scene.

"We were not trained in evangelism, and there was nothing organized. The Renewal came into the school without anyone planning it.

"AIS was a totally secular school, and it was not open for anyone to come and preach. The school had no discipleship program. There was no organization or leadership to what happened. It was just what was welling up from our hearts as we met together to share our experiences with the Lord, day after day, week after week and month after month." [33]

The Renewal changed countless lives. Several of these testimonies are recorded next.

Chapter Eleven

§

What the Renewal Meant to These

The Renewal was marked by the fact that so many young people were completely turned around. While I will not give the real names of those whose testimonies I present here (for there might be, even now, some backlash against them, especially for those who are Jews), these testimonies are of very real people. All except one was Jewish, and all, at the time of their encounter with the Holy Spirit, were under the age of thirty. Today, many years later, their lives are still glowing with what the Holy Spirit has done for them. One of the testimonies is the typical "I-was-in-the-gutter-and-desperate" variety, while the others simply reflect a search for truth.

The first testimony is of this latter type. David (not his real name) was a young Israeli Jew who always had vaguely believed in God, without ever having had a personal experience with Him. He had held many discussions with religious Jews, seeking answers to his questions concerning death, sin and the meaning of life. Then David contracted a strange disease which the doctors could not diagnose. In the hospital, the Book of Psalms was given to him by a fellow patient, an Orthodox Jew. What impressed David about the Book of Psalms was that it was concerned with the same questions that he was asking.

Within a week, his condition had so improved that he was allowed to leave the hospital without the doctors ever knowing what his illness had been. He later attributed his healing to the direct intervention of God. This led David to believe that God hears and cares for us individually.

With this new knowledge that God does hear and answer prayer, David asked the Lord to guide him toward a more complete understanding of His will for his life. This prayer was answered in a rather unusual way.

David served out his compulsory military service and traveled to Europe, finding himself, eventually, in Spain, without money and unable to speak Spanish. He prayed that God would help him find a job and that He would also help him to learn the language. Much to his surprise, he was hired by an encyclopedia company. Against his protests that he did not even speak Spanish, the company assigned him to sell door-to-door. Fortunately, he was to work with another man who was fluent in Spanish. Much to his amazement, David was able to speak passable Spanish within a month and a half. He began to realize that God does answer specific prayers and that He does meet specific needs.

David arrived next in Amsterdam, at a Christian youth hostel, because, he said, "It was the cheapest place to stay." There at this hostel, he met some young people who had found answers to the same questions he had been asking. He quickly realized, however, that these other young people were all Gentiles. As a Jew, he could not see any place for himself in a Gentile faith.

After two months of study in the hostel, it suddenly dawned on David one day that Jesus was a Jew, that His disciples had been Jews and that the New Testament was a Jewish book. "I learned that the New Covenant is a continuation of the former covenant that God established with the Jewish people, that Jesus began His ministry by teaching that He had come only to 'the lost sheep of the House of Israel,' that Jesus had refused, at first, to minister to non-Jews, because, He said, it was 'not fit' to give 'food meant for the children to the dogs.' "

Discovering that Jesus had come primarily for the salvation of the Jews, however, did not resolve David's problem of how he, a Jew, could fit his life into the framework of a Messianic believer. At this point, He met a young Israeli believer who invited him to her house for Bible studies. She told David that it wasn't religion that brought salvation, and that neither the Jewish, the Christian or the Moslem religion brings salvation.

He remembered, "She taught me that Jesus is the way and the only way to salvation, that sin forms a partition between God and man, and that only Jesus, the Messiah, can remove that partition.

"I began to understand that all of history has been part of God's plan of salvation for men. The Torah given to Moses was a part; the sacrifices given in the Temple were a part; and now the plan of God has been brought to its completion in Jesus' death on the cross for our sins. I found that the *Mitsvot* (Commandments) and the Law have their place, but that they are unable to establish a perfect relationship between God and man.

"The New Covenant has brought the Jewish people out from under the yoke of the *Mitzvot* and the Law. I know now that this New Covenant is a direct and natural continuation of the former covenant made with the children of Israel under Moses."

Despite all of this, David had misgivings concerning the break in the relationship with his people he might suffer if he accepted Jesus as Lord and Savior. "I was brought to the point where I just had to face the reality and admit to myself that I had learned so much that was true. So many questions that had worried me had been answered by this knowledge that Jesus was the Messiah, that I just had to make any sacrifice needed to follow Him.

"Then a great thing happened. I began to really understand what Judaism is all about. Instead of being thrust away from Judaism, I was brought back to it. I began to understand the purpose that God has for the Jews, why He brought us back to Israel. I realized that God will give this same truth to all in Israel who will receive it.

"God has brought me back to the faith of Abraham, Isaac and Jacob, and He has done this through His Son and my Lord, Jesus, the Messiah." [34]

Andre (again, not his real name) was not Jewish, but he was married to an Israeli Jewish believer. They had two little daughters and were very active in a congregation of Jewish believers in Kefar Saba. This is his story: "I came to the Lord in Amsterdam. I was traveling, really searching for a deeper meaning to life. I was dabbling in Eastern religions, trying to understand who I was.

"I was twenty-one at the time and was trying anything that would lift me up out of the kind of life I was leading. I was rejecting all religious institutions. Raised in a non-Christian home, I had never been to church in my life. But I was looking for truth and sincerity.

"This search for sincerity brought me into contact with a group of people who I thought at the time had a real spiritual experience. I later learned that what they had was not from God.

"I believed, during this period of my life, that there were many ways to God. I thought that God was in everything. I believed that every religion and every philosophy and even every honest search for God would lead a person to Him. I believed that Buddha and Mohammed and Jesus were all true prophets. This was a very comfortable belief, for it didn't require moral choices of me. Then one day, I met a group of Christian believers in Amsterdam. It happened in this way:

"I was talking with a friend when I noticed a place that had lights and music. I was drawn to it and looked inside. It turned out to be a Christian coffeehouse, though I didn't know that at the time. What I saw was a young man playing the guitar, and the place looked peaceful and quiet, so I went in. After the man finished playing the guitar, some people came over to me, and a young girl among them shared her faith with me, telling me how she had come to accept Jesus as her Lord and Savior.

"I was interested in what she was saying because her life sounded like what I was experiencing myself. She had also been searching and had also dabbled in Eastern religions. She had even gone to India, and along the way she had met a group of believers who had shared their faith with her. The result was that she became a believer.

"What struck me about this young lady was that she didn't preach to me or tell me that I was wrong. She simply gave me her testimony. She was so sincere that I sensed reality behind what she was saying, and I wanted to know more about what she believed.

"The group of young people who ran that coffee bar was called Youth With A Mission, and they invited me to become part of their community. There in their community, I found a way of life that was very different from anything I had ever known. I saw people living together and loving one another. Here was a group of people living together in a deep relationship, in complete harmony.

"For me, this was a great revelation. Suddenly it was clear to me that love was the greatest reality in the world and that I did not have this same love in my life. This caused me to realize, the more that I lived with them, that my whole philosophy was wrong and of no consequence.

"I began to think more and more about Jesus. To me, He had been just one of many ways to reach God. Now I had to consider His words, "I am the Way, the Truth, and the Life; no one cometh unto the Father but by Me." As I thought on those words, I realized that either He was really the only way to God or He was a liar. The claims of Jesus really bothered me, and I had no peace.

"I was unable to get Jesus out of my mind. He didn't fit into my philosophy of life. It was apparent that I had come to a point of decision, and there was a big struggle raging inside of me.

"One day, when I was talking with a friend about my doubts, I dared to say, 'I believe that Jesus really is the only way.' As I said these words, I felt a strong conviction within my spirit that said, 'Yes, what you are saying is right.'

"That day, I experienced for the first time that when you speak truth, it is echoed by the Holy Spirit within you. For me, that was a great revelation. From that time on, I believed that everything that Jesus said about Himself was true.

"Still, I was living my own life, and though I believed intellectually that Jesus was the only way, nothing was changing within me. Slowly, slowly, however, the Holy Spirit began to change me. He did this through people that I met. I could see that they had something I didn't have. The Holy Spirit began to convict me that I was a sinner and showed me that I had been doing wrong. A sense of guilt began to work on me more and more, and I almost came to the point that I didn't want to meet with the Christians. I was so ashamed of myself.

"I stayed away from the believers for about a year, knowing that I had to change, but not knowing what I had to do with Jesus. I knew that I had not only to accept Jesus intellectually, but that I also had to change. I tried to change myself, but it didn't work. I didn't have the power. God had brought me to the point in my life that I was completely broken.

"The last year of my struggle was the hardest. I tried so many things to remove the guilt and self-condemnation, but nothing worked. At one point, I was attending a rock concert, and many cult members were there. I realized that they were nothing but ashes and clay. They had nothing to help me with my needs. It was then that I prayed my first prayer — ever. I asked God to help me.

"When I got back to Amsterdam, I went back to see the believers there. This time, I attended one of their services. There was a great sense of worship in the meeting, and I felt something coming over me. I began to cry. I told God that if He could make me cry, He must be a great God because my heart had been like stone. I hadn't been able to cry for a long time, and here I was crying in public in front of everyone.

"I told the Lord that I wanted to give my life to Him, and I wanted to do everything that He wanted me to do. I told the people around me, 'I want to accept Jesus. I want to be a believer also.'

"People began to pray for me. They encouraged me to pray also, but I didn't know how to pray. They told me not to worry about it, that it would come, to give it time. They invited me to come live with them, and I did. For me, this was the start of my conversion, the changing of my life.

"The first day I was with them, there was another worship service. This time, I found the words to pray, and I accepted Jesus as my Lord and Savior. After that, things happened really fast. God made me sensitive to His voice, and my life began to change dramatically.

"God did another great miracle for me. For the first time in years, I was able to sleep without worrying. It was wonderful. I knew that finally I had made the right choice. I was twenty-one.

"A few months after I had accepted the Lord, I was telling everyone I met about Jesus. I met two Jewish girls from France and told them about my newfound faith. One of them said, 'Well, that is fine for you, but we are Jewish. We don't need Jesus.' This challenged me to search the Scriptures to find out if it was true that there were some people who didn't need Jesus. I didn't find that anywhere in the Bible.

"God gave me a great burden for the Jewish people. After living in that Christian community for a year, I started to work in a Christian hostel in Amsterdam where foreigners came. There and in other parts of the city, I met many Israelis. My heart went out to them, and I told them about Jesus. One of the first Israelis I met also came to the Lord through my witness.

"I received a burden to study Hebrew so that I could read the Bible in the original language and so that I could speak with Israelis in their own language. I had wanted to go to Israel several times before, but nothing had ever worked out. Now, at the hostel, I met a young Israeli girl and she became my Hebrew teacher. Over the coming months, God brought us together in a beautiful way; she later became my wife and we went back to live in Israel.

"Young people are searching. They have not found meaning in the materialism of their parents, and they are looking to Eastern religions and other cults, drugs, sex, Satan worship — anything that promises them meaning in life.

"Even this generation of the past five years is different from my own generation. My generation was actively searching everywhere for meaning to life. Now young people have found that there are no answers to be found in drugs. Now, there is nothing but apathy; young people have given up. They found nothing in acid rock music, in drugs or in the cults, and they have just given up. There is nothing but violence now. So far, this violence in mainly in the States and in Europe, but this violence will probably come to Israel also.

"On the other hand, the young people in Israel

are protected, somewhat, from this hopelessness because of the harshness of life in Israel. They are faced with a continuous state of war, with eighty percent inflation, with the difficulty of making a living here. These harsh realities help them to not be as apathetic toward life as young people in Europe and America." [35]

There was a reason that most of the believers who were caught up in the Renewal were under thirty. Older people had already found themselves, or at least had settled down to endure what life had to offer. This was not true of young people. The young people of the Renewal were finding answers in their experience. They were finding fulfillment, they were finding acceptance, they were finding love, and they were finding fellowship — all the things that make life really meaningful. Young people are always searching for truth, and these young people were finding it in Jesus Christ and in His Word.

Other Israeli young people, those not caught up in the Renewal, had their *havrot* (social groups), but they were not finding in them the meaning for which they were searching. Their groups provided a type of temporary fellowship, but they did not provide the meaningful relationships they needed. Young people need to feel accepted and understood by their peer groups.

There was one more notable common thread shared by these young people. The great majority of them were persons of real need, lonely people who had been wounded by life. Their parents had told them of the horrors of the Holocaust, and consequently they were pessimistic about the future. Many of them hoped to someday leave Israel to seek a better life somewhere else. In times of war, of course, they would return to fight for Israel and to die, if necessary. Although they were anxious to leave Israel, Israeli young people loved their country, fanatically so. No people could love their country more. But they also longed for the opportunities they heard about in America and Europe. Older believers had the task of teaching these young people that true peace can be found only by knowing Him who is the Prince of Peace.

Moshe was a young Israeli who was not only lifted out of sin, but also out of mental illness. He remembers: "I was born on October 26, 1954, in Kibbutz Hulda near Rehovot. When I was eight months old, we moved to my mother's kibbutz, Avelet Hashahar. When I was three, we moved again to Moshav Sde-Moshe, where I lived until I left home at age fifteen.

"I became a hippie. I wasn't happy with people; there was too much hypocrisy. People said one thing, but did another. There were no answers to life. I was rebellious and strong-willed, and I thought that drugs were the answer to everything. When I was 'stoned,' everyone was my friend.

"I left school to live in Eilat, then in Achziv, then in Nuweiba — anywhere I could find hippies. One day I heard about Jesus from a woman who invited me to stay at her house. There was a group of us by then, and we came more for the bed and food than to hear about Jesus.

"As the old woman told us of the prophecies in the Tanakh about the coming of the Messiah, I realized that Jesus was that Messiah, the Messiah of Israel. I came to realize that if God was God and that if Jesus was who the Bible said He was, I would have to give Him everything. I would have to give Him my time, my money and, most of all, myself. I decided I didn't want to do that.

"I went back to my old life — drugs, women, etc. — but it wasn't the same. Somewhere inside I knew what the truth was, and I could no longer be satisfied without it. Still, I ran away from the truth for six years. I traveled through Europe, selling drugs in Amsterdam, begging in France, picking grapes in Italy and being arrested in Holland. From there, I was deported back to Israel.

"Back in Israel, I was arrested for selling hashish, and while I was waiting to be sentenced, I was ministered to by believers. I asked God to help me, and He answered my prayer. I was put on probation.

"Again, I spit in God's face and returned to my old habits. This time, however, I became depressed

— so much so that I tried to commit suicide. I was put in a mental hospital for almost three years. It wasn't so bad. At least, I didn't have to worry about food and shelter. If I wanted drugs, all I had to do was to become violent. Valium would give me several hours sleep without dreams, and that was heaven for me.

"I was dismissed several times from the hospital, but I always went back. Finally, they caught on to my game and threw me out. By this time, my friends had become disgusted with me and would not have anything to do with me. Suddenly, I had no place to go.

"I tried to kill myself again, hoping to be admitted back into the mental hospital, but I was unsuccessful. Something or someone always saved me from dying on these occasions. Once I took over a hundred pills and was unconscious for two weeks, but still I kept on living. I tried to starve myself to death, but even that didn't work.

"All this time, I had kept my Bible with me, but I seldom read it because my understanding was so darkened that I couldn't remember what I had read. Then something unusual happened. For eight straight days, I read the Bible, and it became like a stream of light penetrating my very being. I experienced something I had never known before. Now, I knew that everything was going to be all right. I didn't even pray for inner peace, but it came to me nevertheless.

"I returned to Nuweiba, where there were believers witnessing to the hippies. There, I stayed with a believer who had a tent ministry, and I studied the Bible with him. I found that I could accept Jesus as the Messiah, but not yet as Lord of all. I was still full of bitterness. Life was so hard. My relationships with other people proved to be so painful that I decided to leave for Cyprus and live in a cave near Patmos.

"With money I received from the government for being a paranoid schizophrenic, I bought a ticket for Cyprus. On board the ship were two believers who sang songs all night long. The next morning, I asked them to lead me to the place where I could accept Jesus as Lord. They did. Immediately, Jesus removed all doubt from my heart. I caught the next boat back to Israel. I was now a new creature in Jesus Christ." [36]

Finally, I want to share the testimony of Naomi, a young Jewish Sabra, who sought God through the cults and found Him in the company of Spirit-filled Christians: "My name is Naomi, and today I am twenty-eight years old. I was born in Israel, but my father is from Poland, and my mother is from Egypt. Both of my parents are very frail; life has not been easy for them. They were forced to come to Israel because of Hitler's Holocaust. Israel is very strange to them. All their energy has been consumed in the struggle just to survive. There is always conflict and an empty vacuum in our home. Although my parents love me dearly, in a sense they *'deserted me and the Lord took me up.'*

"I have always had a strong intellectual curiosity about the meaning of life. As a young child, I began to realize that I was somehow different from other children. Other children sensed this difference too, and they persecuted me as a result.

"I studied in school about anti-Semitism, and this caused me to identify strongly with other Jewish people. I learned that people who have 'the stamp of God' upon them are hated by others and are rejected by the world. I hated this difference, wanted to be like everybody else and set about to 'normalize' myself.

"As I strove toward this goal, however, I discovered that there is a horrible satanic power in this world, and it was beginning to overpower me. The devil drove me, more and more, into a corner. I was a thoughtful and impressionable young girl, and I absorbed all the satanic philosophy that was taught to us in school. I was terrified by the Darwinist theory that only the strong survive and the weak perish. I decided that there was no place in the world for me. I began to take psychedelic drugs, which caused me to experience hellish torments.

"At last, God took pity on me and lifted me out of this hell. He healed me and restored me to life. It was like being born again — but not in the Christian sense. I did learn a lot: that life was a supernatural gift not to be taken for granted, that God was alive, that He did love me and that all my existence depended on Him. I decided to dedicate my life to searching for God.

"I left school, deciding to study on my own. I moved to Jerusalem, and there I lived alone. I felt like a small boat tossed about on a stormy sea. Then I met a cultic group which seemed to have an amazing spiritual power and depth. I was convinced that I had found what I was searching for. I did not realize that by studying a mystical philosophy, like the kabbala, I was filling my whole being with darkness.

"Three years later, my involvement with this cult came to an end, when there was a division in the group. However, I was still a devoted follower of the cult and wanted to return to it.

"It was a year after that when the Lord found me. A friend of mine met a Messianic believer on the bus, and this believer invited my friend to attend one of the Messianic meetings. I went along.

"When I arrived at the Messianic worship service, I immediately felt the presence of the Holy Spirit. At that very first meeting, I fell on my knees and declared that Jesus was my Lord. Still, in my heart and mind there was a great struggle going on between the teachings of Satan and the light of God revealed to me through the Holy Spirit. The devil fought me tooth and nail and tore my soul to shreds. I was angry about what was happening to me. God seemed to be leading me into a desert of the shadow of death.

"Two years of this pain ended when I returned to the Lord with my whole heart, broken and humbled. God's love restored my life. From that day, I have not missed a single meeting of the believers, and the Lord has bestowed upon me His blessings without ceasing. He has been faithful to continue to work in me, to break me in different ways. He does this so as to mold me into the image of Jesus, that I might be part of the Body of Christ, the Bride of the Lamb.

"During the four years that I have been in the faith, God has given me verses and passages from the Bible that confirm His love for me and His purpose that He has for my life. I know that I am in His hands and that He truly loves me. I thank Him for His gifts and for His grace. The one great thing that I have asked from Him is that He will give me — and all His Church — the gift of praise. The essence of the life of the redeemed of the Lord is to praise Him." [37]

No area of Israel has had a more exciting movement of the Renewal than the Galilee, described in the following chapter.

CHAPTER TWELVE

§

THE RENEWAL IN THE NORTH

THE RENEWAL IN NORTHERN ISRAEL CENTERED AROUND Tiberias, and two prime figures in the activities of that area are Ken and Marge Crowell.

The Crowells first arrived in Israel in June of 1969, when Ken was under contract with the Motorola Corporation as a manager of research and development. Ken and Marge first attended the home worship services of a Hebrew believer in Ramat Gan, but because they did not know Hebrew and felt that requiring translation of everything into English just for them placed too great a burden on the congregration, they began to attend the services of the Baptist Village congregation.

Ken remembers several of the expatriates who were working among the Jews coming together to seek God's will for their ministries: "We prayed for direction, and out of this came a turning point in my life. We couldn't all be preachers, yet we all wanted to know the direction God would have us move in our ministries.

"There wasn't much going on anywhere in the country at the time, except for individuals who were carrying on their own personal efforts. For instance, a dear brother, Bill York, had a tract work and had covered almost all of the city of Bat Yam with Christian tracts, but the movement of the Holy Spirit had really not started at this time."

The Crowells finished their three-year contract with Motorola in 1972 and returned to the States. But in 1977, they felt that God was pointing them back to Israel, so they returned and settled in Tiberias.

God had given Ken the vision of building a factory in which both believers and nonbelievers could be employed. In response to this, he established "Galtronics," which produced antennas for "walkie-talkies." For instance, the company supplied Motorola with antennas for the sets used by the Israeli police.

A branch of Galtronics was located in Afula. Called "Galcom," it produced long-life batteries. Another branch of the Tiberias company was "Galadon," which produced a nonalcoholic wine. Galadon had its own vines and bottled its own wine. On the label was a picture of Jesus with His disciples at the Last Supper.

Galadon also produced a special unleavened bread made from whole wheat. The two products, the wine and the bread, are used by believers in communion services. These products found a market in the United Kingdom, and Ken began to search for markets in the United States as well.

These business ventures employed thirty-nine workers. Of them, twenty-six were Jewish (but not believers) and thirteen were believers — two of them Arabs.

I take time to describe these business ventures because Ken, a non-Jew and a devout Christian, by establishing an industry which furnished employment to Israelis, had done something unique in the country. While other industries have been established in Israel by non-Jews, some of whom may well be devout Christians (though this writer knows of none), the endeavors of the Crowells seemed unique to me.

The Crowells are unique in another way. Most expatriates go to Israel, serve for a while and then return to their native country. The Crowells chose to become permanent residents of Israel and made Israel their home. Because of that, their witness took on a special authority among the Israelis.

By 1977, the Crowells found that somehow the witness for the Lord in Tiberias had reached a very low ebb. The Church of Scotland Chapel in Tiberias was without a pastor, and the congregation consisted of only four women who met weekly for prayer. Then, things began to happen. Several families, totaling eight persons, moved to Tiberias from various kibbutzim and joined the fellowship. Ken and Marge decided to join the fellowship too, and the little congregation began a period of sustained growth. Rev. Walter Riggins came to be pastor of the little chapel, and his coming furthered the growth.

It was about this time that believers throughout the land began to get a vision of Tiberias becoming the center of what God was doing in the north. The Absorption Center in Tiberias began a process of finding Jews coming to Israel who had had an experience with the Lord overseas. These Jews had met Jesus Christ, but they had no background whatever in the practical issues of forming fellowships or establishing churches. They brought about the first crisis in the little fellowship, when they decided to split off from the non-Jewish believers attending the meetings.

Later, these same Jewish brethren had a change of heart and rejoined the group. God used this incident to teach the Jewish brothers that we are all one in the Lord.

The fellowship also began meeting occasionally with the Baptist Arab congregation that Suhail Ramadan pastored in the Arab village of Tu'ran. Suddenly, Jews, Arabs and expatriates were worshipping God together. By the end of 1977, the group had grown to thirty-five.

In 1978, a leadership of "elders" was established in the fellowship, and Ken was asked to be the head of it. This caused some anxiety. Since he came from a Baptist background, there was some concern that he would attempt to establish a Baptist Church. This feeling disappeared, however, when he encouraged the services to remain free and unstructured. He remembered: "We began in prayer, and our meetings have largely consisted of prayer ever since. There were several in the fellowship who had various gifts of the Spirit, but our meetings have not been what could be called 'Charismatic.' If we feel like raising our hands, we do so, but if we do not feel like raising our hands, we don't. Each person is left to worship as he chooses.

"Sometimes we pray for three or four hours, seeking the will of the Lord. Once, we began to get an impression from the Lord that we were attempting to build on sand. We could not understand what the Lord was trying to tell us. As time went on, we realized that we were trying to please a lot of different people. The passage about the valley of dry bones in Ezekiel 37 was brought to mind. Along with this impression came the thought of the pile of skulls that is shown to tourists visiting the Monastery of Saint Catherine at Mount Sinai. We couldn't understand these images until someone remarked that these skulls piled together looked like grains of sand. God was telling us that all of us were striving to be the head without realizing that the Body of Christ is made up of many parts. When we understood this, we decided to stop the direction in which the fellowship was going and to get back to the foundation, Jesus Christ.

"When we made this change in direction, the fellowship really began to grow. Before, we had been torn apart by different people striving to press for their own ideas. Now, we decided not to do anything unless there was unity.

"One day, as I was praying in our meeting, I received a vision of a snake. In the vision, there appeared a great heel that stepped on the snake and crushed it. God was saying to us that Satan had been defeated and that we were not to hold back in fear anymore. We were to step out in boldness. From that night, we began to stand tall in the boldness of the Lord.

"As the group grew, the number of elders was increased to five. The fellowship, having grown to more than eighty by this time, was now meeting in a hotel. The members of the congregation began to go out into the streets of Tiberias and to witness boldly. Orthodox Jews began to stone the hotel where the fellowship was meeting, and on Christmas Day in 1983, they set fire to the hotel. The fire caused so much damage to the hotel that the owner would no longer allow the believers to meet there.

"The actions of the Orthodox Jews led to meetings with the mayor and with the Chief of Police. Television, radio and newspapers publicized these problems and resulted in the Gospel being spread, not only in Tiberias, but throughout the land and even overseas.

"In 1983, the fellowship began to observe Communion, the Lord's Supper. It was decided not to observe it by some denominational tradition, but simply to consider the wine and the bread as the blood and body of Jesus Christ. The manner of conducting this important service in the life of the church almost became a big issue in the fellowship, but by seeking God's will in love, unity was preserved.

"The elders do not carry through on any decision in which there is not unity. Often, these elders will arrive at a meeting with varying opinions, but almost every time they are able to arrive at complete agreement before leaving.

"Our Communion services are really sweet times. After these services, we often call for those among us who are ill, and we seek healing for them. We have never considered that there are those among us who have the gift of healing; we just pray for the sick and depend on God to do the healing — and

He does. Just last week, there were two little girls in the group who were deaf. We prayed for them, and their hearing was restored. We have seen so many miracles in our meetings."

After being forced out of the hotel, the fellowship began to meet in the forest. Services were held on Saturdays from 4:00 to 6:00 PM, with between a hundred and a hundred and twenty-five attending.

Marge Crowell remembers several women who wanted to have a Bible study in 1980: "There was a problem. We all wanted to be teachers. When we were listening to someone else teach, we were really thinking about when it would be *our* turn to teach. We decided to drop the idea of Bible study and simply pray. Prayer brought us together, and now we have a large group of women who meet once a week for prayer. Once a month, women from all over the country come together to pray. We meet on Monday morning at 9:00 in different homes."

While the group was meeting in the hotel, the children were taught in both English and Hebrew. Now the children who spoke only English have either learned Hebrew or moved away, so only Hebrew is used to teach the children.

As the work grew, four deacons were elected to assist the five elders. The duty of these deacons was to assume responsibility for teaching the children.

Most of the Jews in the fellowship were from overseas, and were under the age of thirty. Most of them were already believers when they arrived in the country.

The Saturday service was just an opportunity for gathering together. There were other meetings, mostly for prayer. Other meetings were also held at night on Sundays, Tuesdays, Wednesdays and Thursdays.

Ken states, "God is making Himself known as the God of Israel in Tiberias today." [38]

It has already been stated that one of the "cycles" of the Renewal was that of persecution. In the following chapter, such a persecution is described.

Chapter Thirteen

§

The Anatomy of a Persecution

The thought of so many Jews worshipping Jesus stirred up many hornets' nests around the country, and persecution set in. Here is an example of what followed for many believers:

"My name is Arieh. My wife and I moved to Rosh Pina from England. I had grown up as an Orthodox Jew, but at the age of fifteen I had turned my back on the Jewish faith. The study of the Talmud had not brought me life, only death. The 'Holy of Holies,' so to speak, was empty. I had left it all and had been searching through different Eastern religions, philosophies and cults.

"Soon after our arrival in Rosh Pina, three believers moved into the house next door. They sang a lot and were very open about their faith in Jesus. They witnessed to me, but eventually gave up on me. Then, suddenly, without my knowledge, my wife, who also is Jewish, accepted Jesus as her Savior. One day, she just said, 'I believe in Jesus. There are now three persons in our life: you, me and Jesus.'

"One Saturday afternoon, about eight months after my wife had become a believer, I said (half in jest), 'What would you think if I gave my life to Jesus?' The moment I said it, however, I realized that I meant it.

"I went next door to tell the brothers, and one of them said to me, 'If I didn't know that you would not lie about something like this, I would not believe you.'

"I prepared myself immediately for water baptism. I renounced all my occult practices, and three weeks later my wife and I were baptized in water. Three weeks after that, we both were baptized in the Holy Spirit.

"By this time, we had been living in Rosh Pina about a year and a half. We had come to know a couple there very well, and we began to tell them about our new faith. It turned out that the man had been having dreams about three men who had come to talk to him, and one of the three men was Jesus.

"I had been working as a tractor driver, but six months after my baptism, I lost my job. This friend that I had been witnessing to was very upset and kept asking me how I was going to support my family. I told him that God would provide for all our needs and that He would lead me into what He wanted me to do. I continued to witness to him and his wife, and eventually they both came to accept Jesus.

"The three brothers I mentioned felt that God wanted our family, another lady who was a believer and themselves to form a community in which we would all share everything. There was to be one bank account, and everyone was to take from it as the need arose.

"Three weeks after I lost my job, the three brothers felt that they should leave their jobs also and trust God for their needs. So, our new community had no one working, no income coming in. We were all trusting God for our needs.

"Miraculous things began to happen. People whom we had never heard of would come to us and tell us that God had told them to give us money. It was not that we were against working or that we did not plan to go back to work when God directed us to do so. It was just that this was a time of testing. This was a time to grow in the Lord and a time of waiting upon Him to direct us as to what paths we should take.

"There were now twelve people living in the community, in a town of only eight hundred people. In Jerusalem, there might have been a thousand believers, but there were a half million people in the city. We thought our ratio of believers to population was a pretty good one.

"We met together once a week for prayer and praise, and more often during the week for fellowship. We had about six months 'grace' before the persecution began.

"In Upper Rosh Pina, there was a section of the town that had the reputation of being a 'hippie center.' Heavy things were going on there: drugs, sex, etc. We met some of the people who lived there, and one lady invited us to her son's bar mitzvah. We went to the service early in the morning, about 8:00, and there were seven men waiting around for a *minyan* (the required ten men) because they could not start the service without ten being present. The three of us made up the *minyan*.

"One of the men asked if any of us was a Cohen (a descendant from the priestly tribe) because only a Cohen or a Levite can read the Law. As it turned out, we were all Cohens, so they gave the oldest of us the honor of reading the Law. They knew that we believed in Jesus because we had been very open about it. By this time, a lot of people had come into the synagogue, and they began to ask why one who believed in Jesus had been given the honor of reading the Law. There was some grumbling, but no one stopped the reading. That service caused a lot of talk around the town and was to cause us problems in the future.

"The local rabbi became so upset about our growing community that he contacted some religious extremists, and in September, 1977, the pressure these extremists began to exert on the community came to a head. Our landlord was warned not to renew our lease. We took the matter to court, and the judge ruled that we did not have to leave or pay fines that the landlord wanted to levy on us. The judge added, however, that if, in the future, he decided that we should leave, we would have to do so.

"One night, my wife received word from the Lord, through scripture, that *'the watchmen must stand guard at midnight.'* We felt that God was warning us that something would happen that very night, so, instead of going to bed, we stood watch outside.

"About midnight, a truck with some thirty yeshiva students arrived in Rosh Pina. They overpowered us and rushed into the house, where they began tearing things off the wall and breaking up the furniture. They were especially incensed by a picture we had on the wall. It was of a fig tree, and the fig tree is a symbol of Israel. Many Jewish believers think that when Jesus said, *'When you see the fig tree bloom, then you will know that the summer is near,'* He meant that when we see more and more Jews coming to the Lord, His Second Coming would be near.

"A week later, there was a demonstration by local residents. The Israeli press was there in force, and their activities against us received countrywide publicity. In the midst of the confusion, some of the brothers went to a back room to pray. My wife was near the breaking point, so I sent her out of town to stay with a friend. Later that night, the rabbi came back with the yeshiva students. They had iron bars, and they intended to break down the doors. They did knock a small hole in the door, but a neighbor persuaded them to leave.

"In November of 1977, we were invited to speak on a television program called 'Behind the Headlines.' The announcer was very antagonistic and insisted on using the name *Yeshu* for Jesus. In Hebrew, it means 'let his name be erased.' Each time the announcer used this term, one of the brothers corrected him. 'No,' he said, 'His name is *Yeshua*, and it means "the salvation of Jehovah."' When the brother would say this, the program was cut off the air for more than a minute.

"The announcer asked us if it was true that Rabbi Grossman of Migdal Haemek (a famous anti-missionary activist) had offered to meet with us. We answered that we had never been approached by anyone in this matter. Apparently, the studio had been given false information. It was later proved that although a few of the people of Rosh Pina had joined in the demonstrations against us, it was the yeshiva in Migdal Haemek that had organized the whole thing.

"The fact is that we had tried to see Rabbi Grossman, but his students had refused to let us talk to him. Finally, we were able to see him, and our conversation was very interesting. He stated that he did not deny that we were Jews, but his fear was that we would try to influence other Jews to become members of Christian churches — thus weakening Judaism itself.

"We told him that we were not members of Christian churches (we just worshipped in our homes) and although we had accepted Jesus as Savior, we were still Jews. We had found what all Jews were seeking — the Messiah. He stated that the persecution had come from Jerusalem, but it was later proved that this was not true. His yeshiva had caused it.

"The combination of the demonstration, the TV program and the accounts in the newspapers caused the situation to be highly publicized, not only in Israel, but all over the world, as well. The pressure from it finally forced my family to move to Nazareth Elite, where we enjoyed a good, warm fellowship with Jewish believers for several years.

"We now live in Jerusalem. I do not know why the Lord has brought us here, but He definitely has a plan for this city. Jewish believers from all over the country are coming here. Many, like ourselves, have been tested already and are better able to face that which is to come." [39]

The future of the Renewal is not without some clouds, some of which are outlined in the next chapter.

§

CHAPTER FOURTEEN

SOME CLOUDS ON THE HORIZON

THE CHURCH IN ISRAEL FACES AN UNCERTAIN FUTURE; IT always has. As the saying goes, "God doesn't have any grandchildren." In other words, each generation must prove faithful. The Renewal gave the Church a great boost, and perhaps the momentum gained by it will be enough to carry the Church in Israel through adolescence and into maturity.

Although the future of the Church in Israel is uncertain, however, it is not dark. The most pessimistic forecast can only be gray. There are too many signs of healthy vitality in the Church to warrant despair. There are, however, several movements and changes that have puzzled the believers there. There are also a few clouds on the horizon.

There has come, for instance, a definite closing of the era dominated by expatriates active in the Renewal. Only one of the four original families that formed the prayer group at Dugith in the late 1960s is still in the country. In addition, many of the expatriates in the rest of the country, including both of the pastors of the congregations listed in chapter five, are no longer on the scene. Many of these leaders have retired, one of them has died and others have been called to other fields.

One wonders who will replace these and if those who come after will be able to adjust to Renewal conditions. Will there be an attempt by newcomers who have not experienced the changes brought about by the Renewal to again retreat behind denominational barriers? Will they seek to impose their traditional religious values on a Church that is now marching to a different drummer? Will there be an appreciation for a style of worship that differs considerably from their own? Will they be content to assume "followship" roles and be led by local believers who are busy building a Church which is like nothing they have experienced before? Will the desire among these new expatriates to be "chiefs" rather than "Indians" be too strong to resist? If these dangers should materialize, the pre-Renewal atmosphere would not be long in returning. Walls would again go up, and a great chasm would separate believers, as before.

Indeed, there are already signs of walls being rebuilt. Some Roman Catholics, it appears, have been called back behind their barricades by their superiors. There is no longer the same freedom of worship (devoid of doctrinal strings) between Protestant and Catholic that existed for a season.

Also, the Arab Anglican community now seems to be more reluctant to participate fully with other Christian groups. There hasn't been a representative from that body to the annual UCCI (United Christian Council In Israel) meeting in several years.

If, however, new expatriates arrive humble enough to learn from those who may lack their theological training but who have been tested by fire and have been found faithful, then the future of the local church will be bright indeed. Those of us who have lived through the Renewal have learned that the local believers sincerely want us to be part of their communities, and this is a very blessed thing.

A second cloud on the horizon is that inside Israel itself, God seems to be taking a great number of believers out of their fellowships in towns scattered throughout the land, to congregate in Jerusalem. The groups in Natanya, Beersheva, Tiberias, Tel Aviv and elsewhere have all seen members leave for Jerusalem. The number of those departing is so large that the local believers can only come to the conclusion that God is moving His people for a purpose. What this purpose is has not yet been revealed.

But what about the fellowships that are being depopulated? Will they survive? Will they be easier targets for the anti-Christian forces that seem to be gathering strength?

This timidity, however, is overshadowed by certain strong and healthy signs in these fellowships. If the expatriates, at least those who were active in the Renewal, have left, their places of leadership have been taken over by the local believers themselves. This can only bode well for the future. There is an indigenous Church taking root in the land, and this is an answer to the prayer of everyone who ever served there.

This new thing, this indigenous expression, abhors labels of any kind — sometimes even the term "Christian" itself. This is unsettling to some. The Lord Jesus Christ, however, is lifted up in the midst of the people, and the Holy Spirit frequents their gatherings. Against such evidence of God's hand on His people, the uninitiated would do well to keep silent.

Such clear demonstrations of strength in the Church reduce future dangers to the status of problems, and problems have solutions. Finding solutions brings feelings of self-reliance. When this self-reliance is based on obedience to God (and the Body of Christ in Israel is taking great pains to obey Him), and when this self-reliance is based on the guidance of the Holy Spirit, surely the gates of Hell must begin to quake.

Still, we must pray for the believers in Israel. They are still a relatively small minority. It is only by remembering what the Christian community looked like before the Renewal that the present number seems so large. We should pray for the existing fellowships, that God will bless them, but then, He obviously is.

Gentle rains (blessings) continue to fall upon the believers in Israel. Some of these blessings are related in the following chapter.

Chapter Fifteen

§

Continuing Latter Rains

IN SURVEYING THE CURRENT SITUATION OF THE CHURCH in Israel, most of what has already been cited still applies. More fellowships have sprung up throughout the land in recent years, and the older ones continue to grow. The Renewal continues, perhaps with a little less exuberance, but at least there has been no return to the deadness that had prevailed previously.

Almost every training facility in the country is busy striving to meet the demands of those who want to know more about the Lord. The commitment of those who have received the Lord Jesus Christ as their Savior does not appear to be superficial.

Even many who are not part of the Charismatic Movement have been blessed by this move of the Spirit and render appreciation for its fruit. Joe Shulam, pastor of the Netivyah (The Way of the Lord) fellowship in Jerusalem makes an interesting observation: "I believe that there were a great number of Jewish believers in Israel before the Renewal who were too timid to make their presence known. After the large numbers of Jewish believers came into the country during the late 1970s, those believers already here gained the courage to come forward and express their love for Christ. They now had the fellowship and moral support of other believers, and they happily joined the budding fellowships.

"I am convinced that the Jewish believers in Israel will become less and less 'Christian' (at least as the Western countries have experienced Christianity), but they will become more and more 'Christ-like.' This growing difference in the Jewish believers will not serve to drive them further away from their non-Jewish brothers and sisters. On the contrary, as both Jews and non-Jewish believers in Jesus share their strengths, the Body of Christ in Israel will become stronger."

Another source of "latter rain" from the Renewal has been the drawing together and closer cooperation between Arab and Jewish believers. One could cite many such instances, but I offer two:

Salim Ramadan is the son of Suhail and Fida Ramadan of Tu'ran, where Suhail is the pastor of the Tu'ran Baptist Church. Each year, the Jewish believers have gatherings during the Passover and Succoth holidays. In these gatherings, Salim leads the singing.

When the group of Jewish believers in Tiberias were burned out of their meeting room in the local hotel, they, at the invitation of the Ramadans, held their services in the church in Tu'ran. This was the impetus for a custom among the Tiberias believers of traveling to other churches in the Galilee to worship with Arab believers.

Ibrihim Sim'an is a Baptist pastor living in Haifa. He was the first Arab to be employed by the Israeli government in the Ministry of Religious Affairs, Christian Division. Since the Yom Kippur War, Sim'an has carried on a relief ministry for the refugees from Lebanon. Though no longer employed by the government, Sim'an continues to move in both Jewish and Arab circles. In the congregation in Haifa, where Sim'an is pastor, both Jews and Arabs worship together.

The Renewal has brought into Israel, for the first time, enough Christian workers so that the work need no longer exist "on a shoestring." This has resulted in a marked loss of timidity among Jewish believers. The indigenous Church that is emerging in the land one fellowship at a time is being built on the Rock that is Jesus Christ.

More expatriates will go to Israel. May they, as they see such vitality among the believers, read this and not suppose that it was always so. There are signs of a great spiritual revival in the land, and though this writer's contribution has been tiny and inconsequential, I am grateful that the Lord allowed me to witness its beginnings. It is a thing of some importance to me to be able to say, "I was there; I saw Him; I felt His presence; and it changed me."

Postscript

I retired from Israel in 1989, but I have returned four times to update this account of the Renewal. For the most part, I was greatly encouraged by what I saw. The little Baptist chapel in Jerusalem that had been burned down has been replaced by a much larger and more beautiful church building. Whereas the service in the former chapel had been in English, today there are two services — one in English and the other in Hebrew. Both services are well attended.

Dugith, the art gallery and book store in Tel Aviv, now has a prominent sign, "Messianic Bookstore," which bravely informs the public that Jews who have accepted Jesus Christ as Savior are in charge. The Baptists have turned the gallery over to Jewish believers, who have taken full responsibility for maintaining it and are succeeding. By presenting to the Israelis the proof that Jewish believers can mount an indigenous project, they have served notice that they are also in the marketplace of Israeli life.

Believers in Tiberias are growing in every way — including financially. Ken and Marge Crowell, leaders in the group from the beginning, have seen the group grow to more than two hundred. Finding a place to meet has become a problem.

Also in Tiberias, the Crowells have built a tourist attraction on the shore of the Sea of Galilee. Daily, they show a beautiful film of the history of the Sea of Galilee, with an emphasis on Jesus' connection with the sea.

The Beit Immanuel congregation in Joppa-Tel Aviv continues and has served as a source for sending out leaders for the eight other congregations located around the city.

The Baptist Village, near Petach Tikva, with the largest accommodations, continues to serve for the mass meetings of the little congregations throughout the country.

There are thirty-four small Jewish congregations in the country, with the largest being four Roman Catholic congregations (with more than fifteen hundred members). There are, in addition to the existing congregations, an unknown number of house groups (some meeting several times a week) spread throughout the country.

For someone coming from the United States, with its glut of churches and millions who attend them, these numbers will hardly be impressive. It will only be those who remember the little handful of believers in Israel a scant twenty years ago who will view this growth in its true perspective and consider it miraculous.

The future of the Jewish believers in Israel appears

to me to be very bright. There are several reasons for this optimism. The first is the great influx of Russians who are flooding into the country. A surprisingly high percentage of these Russian Jews are already believers. They eagerly seek out other believers and populate their meetings. In the future, these Russian Jews, who have already been trained in "faith survival" through the persecution they withstood in Russia, will bring a robust witness to the cause of Christ in the land.

The second reason for my optimism is the longevity of the Renewal itself. Often, perseverance wears down opposition and brings a feeling of grudging acceptance. Time, I believe, is on the side of the believers.

Thirdly, the conduct of the believers themselves has given pause to the secular Jews. After all, these believers are Jews too, and Israel is their country also. They serve in the Israeli Army, often with distinction, a fact not overlooked by those Israelis who have to serve, often to die (while the Orthodox refuse to serve).

In fact, Orthodox Jews still refuse to accept that Israel even exists at all as a nation. The land, in their thinking, will be established by the Messiah, so they consider the present Israel to be "goyish." The Orthodox are a powerful force in Israel, even though they number less than eighteen percent of the population, because they are tightly organized (a good example of the dedicated few being able to control the majority). Their dozen or so seats in the Knesset are vital for either Labor or Likud to gain control and govern successfully. At the same time, there is a disgust toward the Orthodox among secular Israelis, and this will surely some day lessen their hold over the country.

Fourthly, in 1992, the fifteen-year rule of the Likud Party came to an end, with the much more liberal Labor Party coming to power. Even after the much-admired Yitzhak Rabin was assassinated, the motion he set in place for the peace process has continued (and, please God, may it finally succeed). It was an ill-kept secret in Israel that King Hussein of Jordan would have followed Egyptian President Anwar Sadat's peace agreement in a heartbeat, if not for the pressure he felt from Syria and its leader, Hafiz al-Assad. Now, both of these leaders are gone. King Hussein's son is Western-oriented, and will, in all probability, follow his father's lead.

If nothing else, Egypt will continue the truce with Israel (due to economic reasons). Lebanon has ceased to be a viable country in its own right, and it exists today only as a puppet state of Syria. The last obstacle, then, is Syria, and hopefully a few face-saving gestures like the return of the Golan Heights might be enough to bring that country to the table.

If peace with the Arabs does come, the situation of the Jewish believers can only improve. There should be less pressure on them, and the lack of crisis should cause a weakening of the Orthodox influence on government. Someone, however, has cautioned, with the oft-quoted statement of Golda Meir: "Israel can only remain united under pressure. If there was not a crisis facing the country, we would have to invent one."

Finally, it costs something for a Jew to accept Jesus Christ as Savior. There is pressure on the Israeli who has taken that step that most Christians in America have never experienced. The result of this testing is a vital, strong faith which is no stranger to storms. If the Jew, simply by being a Jew, has gained a reputation for stubbornness and tenacity, then the Jewish believer, with that same stubbornness (coupled with a life-changing experience with the Lord Jesus Christ), is not likely to disappear from the landscape.

ENDNOTES

1. According to figures from the Israeli Ministry of Religion.
2. 2 Timothy 3:5, KJV.
3. A Baptist-owned art gallery and bookstore which the author managed for twenty-five years. *Dugith* means "little fishing boat."
4. Jesse C. Fletcher, *Baker James Cauthen, A Man for All Seasons,* Broadman Press, Nashville, 1977.
5. English translation by Ronald G. Smith, Charles Scribner's Sons, New York, 1958.
6. English translation by Norman P. Godhawk, The Macmillan Co. New York, 1952.
7. Donald A. Hagner, in his book, *The Jewish Reclamation of Jesus,* Académie Books, The Zondervan Corporation, Grand Rapids, 1984. Hagner has included extensive listings of these books by Jewish authors during this period.
8. Ibid., p. 273
9. Ibid., p. 274.
10. *My Personal Pentecost,* edited by Roy S. and Martha Koch, Herald Press, Scottsdale, Pennsylvania, 1977, p. 235.
11. A tape received March 6, 1985.
12. Ibid.
13. *My Personal Pentecost,* op. cit., p. 76.
14. Ibid., p. 241.
15. Tape, op. cit.
16. *Masterlife,* a discipling course compiled by Dr. Avery T. Willis, Jr., and published through the Church Training Department of the Sunday School Board of the Southern Baptist Convention. *Masterlife* teaches that God provides as many gifts as there are needs to be met.
17. Op. cit., p. 27.
18. Tape, op. cit.
19. Op. cit., p. 25.
20. Tape, op. cit., p. 27.
21. Interview with Swarr, April 1985.

22. Interview with Lindsey, June 1985.

23. Interview with Register, June 1985.

24. Ibid.

25. Interview with Laty, June 1985.

26. Lindsey, op. cit.

27. Representatives of the Elim Assemblies (Pentecostal) in England. Tiller served in Jerusalem. He is now deceased.

28. The "movement" here means the Charismatic Movement rather than the Renewal per se as described in this writing. (Ed.)

29. From an unpublished paper by Tiller.

30. Material concerning the Sebastians is from an interview, September 1985.

31. The expression "Tabernacle of David" appears in Amos 9:12. In Hebrew, however, the text reads, *Succah David* (booth of David), rather than tabernacle (*mishcon* or *ohel moed* in Hebrew). For this reason, Rashi and other Jewish commentaries interpret the word for tabernacle *Malchoot David* (kingdom of David). Thus the meaning is symbolic, meaning the realm of David rather than a structure. This interpretation, moreover, would stress the point that Loden is making. He is drawing a distinction between the Tabernacle of Moses, with its solemn ritual, and the realm of David, which was marked by joy and praise.

32. The Hebrew word, *avodah* means both "worship" and "work." Luke 2:49 in the King James Version has *"be about my Father's business,"* i.e., "work." Many other translations have *"in my Father's house,"* i.e. "worship."

33. Interview with anonymous student.

34. Interview with "David," June 1985.

35. Interview with "Andre," June 1985.

36. Interview with "Moshe," June 1985.

37. Interview with "Naomi," June 1985.

38. Interview with Ken and Marge Crowell, May 1985.

39. Interview with Arieh, June 1985.